# Michael's Sword & You

# Michael's Sword & You

## *With Archangel Michael*

## Mary Soliel

Boulder, Colorado

# Michael's Sword & You

With Archangel Michael

The author of this book does not dispense professional
advice or prescribe the use of any technique as a form of
treatment for physical, emotional, mental, or medical
problems without the advice of a physician. The intent of
the author is only to offer information to help you in your
own quest for overall well-being. In the event you use any
of the information in this book for yourself, which is your
constitutional right, the author and the publisher assume no
responsibility for your actions.

Twelve Twelve Publishing, LLC books may be ordered
through booksellers or Amazon.com.

**Twelve Twelve Publishing, LLC**
P.O. Box 7208
Broomfield, CO 80021 U.S.A.
**alighthouse@mac.com**

Cover Photo Design: Karen Kliethermes

Logo Design: Lisa Kubik

Because of the dynamic nature of the Internet, any Web
addresses or links contained in this book may have changed
since publication and may no longer be valid.

ISBN: 978-0-9890169-2-6

This book
is dedicated to
you spiritual warriors
whose mission is
Love.

# Contents

Acknowledgments
Author's Note
Introduction

Chapter One:
Introduction to the Sword..................................1

Chapter Two:
The Pilgrimage to Canada ............................ 23

Chapter Three:
Processing the Sword's Power .......................... 47

Chapter Four:
Michael's New Call ........................................ 67

Chapter Five:
Invitation to the Sword .................................. 115

Chapter Six:
Working with the Sword ................................ 123

Chapter Seven:
The Big Eye ............,..................….......…... 137

Chapter Eight:
The Aware Warrior & Self-Care ......…........... 165

Afterword ......................................…........ 209
About the Author ............…..…................... 211

# Acknowledgments

My heart is always in deepest gratitude to beloved Archangel Michael, our powerful, compassionate, most loving Divine being who is here for every single one of us. He is empowering us like never before with the gift of his sword of Light, for the sake of all life and our sacred planet. His love for us cannot be adequately defined or described, only felt. It is the honor of my life to have this connection to him, a connection that we are all invited to have. And we are now invited to work with him, side by side.

My immense gratitude to Jeannie Barnes, my friend and Angel Channeler who helped me to better understand and validate our work with the sword through her own profound messages from Michael. Her role in this book is most significant, as readers will soon see. With her whole heart, she gave of her time and gifts without expecting anything in return—a genuine, altruistic human angel.

With heart-felt thanks to Rhonda Ann Clarke who heard the call from Michael to gather, and with excitement supported me and this mission in an unforgettable pilgrimage together at Lake Louise and Moraine Lake in Canada. This trip helped spawn this very book and brought much joy to each of our lives.

My deep appreciation to Mia Filatov, who wisely and lovingly channeled key concepts and provided stunning validations at the most perfect times—all relevant to Michael's new mission with us. She is a profoundly magical and mystical influence in my life and an important part of this sacred journey.

Always my profound love and appreciation to my beautiful children and all those wonderful friends mentioned in previous books who continue to be of loving support.

Finally, to the readers of my books over the last ten years who continue to be of immense support of my work, and who may choose to join us with Michael on the spiritual front lines of making a difference in the world. There are no words to express my gratitude. We "met" for a reason. I am most excited to begin working with you in a new and most profound way.

# Author's Note

Some names of individuals and a few identifying details have been changed to honor their privacy.

Please also note that this book has not been professionally edited to preserve the authenticity of the messages from Archangel Michael without the lesser concern of perfect grammar. Channeling the Heavenly realms is a most natural process, and I receive just as I speak, not perfectly, but with perfect intentions to bring forth wisdom with clarity and truth.

Further, this book was written with great urgency, having completed it in just three months. With my four other books, it took roughly a year each to accomplish the same. Thus, 3D concerns fell by the wayside. Thank you in advance for your understanding.

~ Mary Soliel

# Introduction

Today is October 2, 2017. Twenty-three years ago, on this very day, a Divine white Light came into my right eye and changed me forevermore. Seven years later, I began to channel messages from Archangel Michael about our new Earth, a Heaven on Earth that we are co-creating. I've previously published four books; two written with Michael. For the past several months, I was experiencing some very intense challenges and an unexpected lull in my work. And then everything shifted completely.

I just spent several days at Michael's vortex centered in Lake Louise, in Alberta, Canada. He led me here. And it was in the midst of this most pristine and heavenly beauty of Western Canada, in the powerful and tangible energy of Archangel Michael, that I came to a life-altering conclusion.

When I approached the reflecting aquamarine brilliance of what I now name the "Diamond Vortex" at Moraine Lake, pictured on the next page, and as I was literally taking pictures of it, that's when everything came into immediate view. I received a rapid understanding that I would write this very book and this image would serve as its cover. I had a clear understanding of what the book would be about: Michael's sword. And it directly involves you. It couldn't be more clear that Michael fully orchestrated this unexpected trip to provide the inspiration for my third channeled book with him, and that it would hold extreme importance.

The following is Archangel Michael's introductory message, provided on this very day, halfway through my pilgrimage to Canada when visiting Kelowna, British Columbia:

*The gap in time between books through this channel was very intentional. There was so much information that needed processing and time to incorporate into your lives. You have now entered new territory. You have passed a finish line of sorts. I am talking to those of you feeling drawn to this book who have done the work or walk this intended path to self-awareness as the change makers.*

*Yes, change makers you are! All of what is developing and evolving could not happen without you. Your efforts are not going unnoticed and have had a monumental effect on the whole. You see, you came here with extraordinary abilities, you are doing so much by just being, just holding the space during these times. Do you get an idea of just how powerful you are that you can simply be in a space and make positive change happen? This is so.*

*Some of you can see or perhaps sense what is going on behind the scenes. Such as when you feel led somewhere and light codes are pouring through you. And you wonder why you are tired, why you feel "burned out" and cannot accomplish much. The fact is you are accomplishing greatness. You are anchoring in great amounts of Light and most likely without realizing it. This channel wonders why she has so many moments of pause in her thinking, seeming forgetfulness, and she sometimes cannot hold onto a thought. It is because she and many of you are filters for the Light. And it has been going on for some time. You so often feel that only part of you is on Earth. You don't know where the rest of you is, but it is not grounded in 3D on Earth.*

*This is courageous work. You know you are in service, and on a deep soul level you offer such a great deal of energy to help the greater good. So much is not as it seems. So much is not as it seems! We revere you for your trust and faith in this new Earth that is fast approaching. You see signs of it, some of you even on a daily basis; you witness the veil lifted further back as the magic of the universe is further illuminated. This is a key word for these are illuminating times. The Light is revealing great truths that have been hidden regarding both the Heavens and the Earth and what has been taking place.*

*And so, you will relish every truth, even when it's difficult to digest, because the truth will free all living things. All that embodies a spirit will be gifted with truth that will free it. And as you move further into your souls, all will become further illuminated and you will be, for the first time, beings who are truly free. Because you never have been so on this planet.*

Archangel Michael extends a most significant invitation to you with this second introductory message for this very book, also while in Kelowna:

*Dear travelers on this journey to the new and Heavenly Earth. You who knew to pick this book to read is no mistake. It is not something of little importance either. It was destined that you read and understand the messages in this book as it will prove to be a most important part of your journey but also the journey of Earth's new path.*

*You see, we are at a turning point both on Earth and in the Heavens. What most people are unaware of is that the battles between Light and dark energies have been ongoing. Yes, in the Heavens too. Not in all planes of the Heavens, of course, as the dark is unable to reach the high planes. But in the lower planes, yes, the battles have been fought in an energetic way. Not as battles are waged on Earth.*

*Just as many of you may feel, these kinds of words and thinking have always made this channel uncomfortable, but she now sees it all differently. The task at hand is to release the clamps of darkness that have plagued humanity and all living things including the Earth herself. All beings feeling the call are now stepping up to this task and I ask if this includes you. Are you willing to face the reality of darkness on your planet and stand only for the Light?*

*I cannot emphasize strongly enough that along with your choice to serve, you must embrace trust and faith, and where fear has no place. If you see all of this from a fearful stance, it will not serve yourself or the cause. You simply must come from a place of love knowing that love truly does conquer all. If you hold fear, the dark has a hold on you. We are asking you to come from a place of immense resolve to serve the greater good and trusting this high call into spiritual warrior work.*

*Now let me talk about the sword. The sword is Light. It represents the power of the Heavens. You can use your imagination to understand the power of the sword. You are being offered the use of my sword for uses I will soon describe. But let this be a warning to those who have other than honorable intentions. There will be no power to the sword if used for dark purposes, if used to harm or influence others' lives or aspects of life that are not to be tampered with. My sword is to be used for only the highest of purposes—three purposes—and they are for Light, Truth, and Protection.*

# Chapter One

## Introduction to the Sword

The year of 2017 was full of surprises. Most were not happy ones but they were just what I needed to prepare for the next stage of my work and the very messages in this book. Having traveled extensively over a period of five months in late 2016, I had returned home just days prior to the new year. For weeks, I was on a traveler's high after having gone with the wind to just where I was led to: Brazil, South of France, Italy, Slovenia, Spain, and Belize. And here, I had not traveled outside of the country (other than Canada) since 1985.

Just when at the height of my life and work in so many ways, my bliss took a drastic turn in the early part of the year. Please bear with me as the following must be addressed as briefly as possible from the start to share the unexpected and most challenging way that this book came into being, and how I was prepared for it. It serves as an example of how to understand and appreciate how Divine forces prepare us for our growth, our work, and our soul's destiny. I also share this to reveal an example of the how and why things happen and how we can accept and transmute even the darkest of experiences and bring them into the Light.

The fact is I experienced my first direct, conscious dance with darkness when I found myself being professionally sabotaged, which bled heavily into both my work and personal life. In addition to my Lightwork, my health, well-being, finances, feelings of security, and more were all deeply affected. The ramifications ran deep and yet it happened for several reasons. I did unequivocally learn one of my greatest life lessons—to trust my intuition which was screaming at me and it was right on! But I did not follow it.

Even as everything was happening, I both strongly sensed and was also told that this occurred for higher reasons that I would not yet understand. Sure enough, I found over time that while a horrific experience to say the least, I needed to go through this to prepare for the position I was to take now— that of an active spiritual warrior on a mission of Love with Archangel Michael by my side. More importantly, I'm being positioned as a human guide for those hearing the call to join this vital mission, and why you may hold this book in your hands. Together, we shall become strong, resolute warriors who will yield an unstoppable force of Light.

There were dark influences that "messed" with me, and continue to try even as I write this book. They were influencing my events and classes, for example. I was told they did not like my Light, they don't like my connection to Archangel Michael, and they were trying to sabotage me—various people in different life situations who I would later learn are curiously and somehow connected.

From several sources, I learned that many true Lightworkers are experiencing the very same and with varying levels of understanding of what is really going on behind the scenes. I'm still learning, and while this is not an enjoyable subject, it is a necessary subject to address as it fully relates to the big story of what we are facing as a whole in the macrocosm.

Thanks to Archangel Michael helping me, I am stronger than ever now, and actually due to what I endured. I have been thrust into spiritual warrior mode as a being of Light, and it was these heart-wrenching experiences that made this possible. Without knowing it, I was in training to both experience and then teach the spiritual warrior way with Archangel Michael.

This book also serves to bring forth awareness of what is really going on in the big picture. There is a battle between Light and dark occurring on Earth *and* in the Heavens. When I first heard that, I realized just how much I don't know. Battles in Heaven are not something I ever thought of, nor envisioned. As I eventually understood, with the many dimensions of Heaven, the battles can only occur on the lower levels. As above, goes below, and these battles are indeed really happening, *but* as we know, the Light wins... Light is love and love always wins in the end.

In short, this is the driving force of this book. These times call for action, not complacency. The Earth and the Heavens need us now, *all of us* willing to step up our roles in the transformation of our planet. It is those of us who are choosing love, truth, and ultimately Light who are being called. We are the truth seekers learning to live from our hearts by deepening our connection to our souls, and while heeding an inner and unshakable call to shift this Earth.

*Michael's Clarion Call: Messages from the Archangel for Creating Heaven on Earth[1]* was my first channeled book with Michael, and this book could technically be called *Michael's New Clarion Call* because Michael is sounding a new call, and it is an urgent and most empowering one. Michael's sword of Light is the cornerstone of his plea.

Since channeling Michael these past sixteen years, most of our work together, including our prior two books, has enlightened readers about the creation of our new Heaven on Earth. But there was a piece of this story that was not ready to be shared until now. We need to step into our new roles as we take action with our free will as peaceful spiritual warriors creating the necessary shift into our new, higher dimensional Earth. My understanding is that this is the most powerful action we can take now,

---

[1] Soliel, Mary. *Michael's Clarion Call*. Boulder: Twelve Twelve Publishing, LLC, 2011.

and it also demands a great deal of faith. Just as most of us cannot (yet) see Archangel Michael, we know that he is around us. And just as we may not always see the immediate effects of our spiritual warrior work, it is very real.

To do this work, we must bravely face reality, not only of the macrocosm, but of the microcosm of our lives, as well. Many Lightworkers are not at all aware that there are increasing dark influences mixing in with the spiritual or what is more commonly known as "New Age" communities. (For the record, I never really aligned myself with the term "New Age" because of certain connotations attributed to it—I see my work as simply "spiritual.") There are people, through their channelings, gatherings, events, websites, etc., posing to be something they are not. Thus, there is much misinformation out there *designed to confuse.*

However, we all can tap into our inner wisdom and intuition, which can temper this. One primary tactic to be aware of is that the unenlightened mix truths in here and there which captures their faith but only to hook them in, among key falsities to serve their goals. We are all seeking to understand so much now, and thus we all can be vulnerable to this. Therefore, exercising constant discernment is absolutely essential now.

As I have said many times to my readers and event participants, we must discern everything, and that certainly includes me and my work, to discern what information comes through me. I discern everything, including all that I receive from Michael to make sure I am hearing correctly, while always seeking validation on anything I desire. While I am human and far from perfect, my unrelenting intention is to always provide absolute truth and clarity to the very best of my ability.

Once Metatron came through with the following message when I was in the midst of coping with big time interference: *You must NOT give the dark influences energy. When they play their games, you must ignore and see them for what they are! This Will Pass, I promise you. They will see you are less and less affected. So, the quicker you lessen that hold, the quicker they go away.*

Archangel Michael explained it to me this way, during that time: *There is always truth mixed in with lies and deception, for that is how the dark works. They lead you in and then grab you, just as your friend described, as in her spider web example. But you got yourself out of their web. And you must know how that was not just a win for you, but also for the Light.*

This makes me also think of words from Michael that speak much louder now than they did when he spoke them years ago, as seen in *Michael's Clarion Call*:

*You who are on Earth are presently being bombarded with dishonesty and untruths coming from so many directions that you often do not know what to believe about earthly things, let alone spiritual ones...this will change.*

So, as I discuss this subject with you, please consider this with detachment. See these as games being played, and we must stay above them but with awareness. The fact is, there is much channeled material out there that inspires people to actually be complacent. The messages influence many that we simply trust that everything is going to magically change, but the truth is we have free will and must listen to our hearts and souls, calling us into action.

We cannot shift this world by merely sitting in the lotus position and sending love and Light. There are plenty of us who have and continue to do this, and of course it helps, however the Earth and its inhabitants continue to be greatly challenged and harmed. And it's getting much more intense now, as duality grows yet further out of balance. Therefore, complacency has not worked and is absolutely not the answer.

To quote these wise beings:

"The world is a dangerous place to live; not because of the people who are evil, but because of the people who don't do anything about it."
~ Albert Einstein

"He who passively accepts evil is as much involved in it as he who helps to perpetrate it. He who accepts evil without protesting against it is really cooperating with it."
~ Martin Luther King, Jr.

"You assist an evil system most effectively by obeying its orders and decrees. An evil system never deserves such allegiance. Allegiance to it means partaking of the evil. A good person will resist an evil system with his or her whole soul."
~ Mahatma Gandhi

The world needs us now and the Heavens are calling us into action in many ways. We all have our areas of interest, passion, and expertise. And yes, some shifts will Divinely occur in the blink of an eye, when we reach the necessary tipping point, but we cannot just be listless, hopeless, or keep our heads in the sand. This book is a call for those sent here to be spiritual warriors of love. This Earth needs every single one of us now, to respond to this call.

On June 16, 2016, Michael provided the following message for me:

*Oh, how we admire your courage and that of many other Lightworkers also feeling this vital call to go "out on a limb," as you say. You MUST take action. You are RIGHT to do so. We are so proud of you and supporting you and PROTECTING you every step of the way. Know this. Know how well things are being played out now BECAUSE of the Lightworkers. You are all making the difference and this cannot be done without you. Oh, there will be celebration when the Light proves it has won. It is a spiritual battle, Mary, as you were thinking this morning.*

Michael almost always comes through so gently, rarely so "loudly" as denoted by the capital letters, so I could feel the significance of this message. I responded: "I feel this is why you wanted me to watch *Joan of Arc* months ago."

*Indeed, for you are among the Lightbearers stepping it up in this role to bring awareness that will free the world to shift into the higher frequencies. What could be more important?*

After months of healing from some deep wounds, I met with my friends Lee and Joe who told me about a shaman they both worked with. Lee is also deeply connected to and works with Archangel Michael, so it was no surprise that he became a part of this story. I instinctively felt I needed to see her, to further transmute the pain of betrayal—one of my core life lessons and thus lessons I was still "attracting." But Michael was up to something much more significant. He was clearly orchestrating this meeting, as I'd soon find out.

I scheduled an appointment for August 4, 2017 (not realizing at the time that it was a 22 master day, for those interested in numerology). What I ended up receiving was not so much a healing but something entirely unexpected. I received a new direction in my spiritual work, and a most significant piece of the grand unfolding that has taken place over months, and which led to this very book—with just one simple and yet profound message. And it was this message and direction that actually healed me over the next several months.

Just minutes after we began the session, the shaman announced that Archangel Michael was here with us.

She said that *Michael put his sword into the ground,* right before me!

He said that while I listen to him so well and have shared his messages just as he has wanted, there is one thing I haven't done. I was surprised by this statement and couldn't wait to understand. And then I heard words that came as quite a surprise.

*You have refused to pick up the sword.*

Michael said I have to learn the ways of the righteous warrior.

Indeed, I was always rejecting the sword. Not that he ever actually asked me to pick it up, but I just naturally rejected it as I shun all instruments of violence. Like many others, I absolutely despise war and violence more than anything.

Further, I never liked depictions of Michael with the sword because that was not how I ever saw him, with the exception of those many times I asked him to help me cut energetic cords. I saw him as this most wise, powerful being filled with the greatest unconditional love and compassion for all, not holding something that represents a possible tool of violence. But in those moments, everything changed. I began to see the sword in a completely different way—always as an instrument of protection, yes, but now as a most necessary instrument of Light.

The irony was that one of things I wanted to heal in this session was the more intense side of my personality. While I am very maternal and gentle, I also have a more intense "let's get to the root of the matter" Scorpio way about me. In recent years, and with some distressing challenges, I noticed that the intense side of me became more prevalent in order to ultimately protect my heart from more pain—and yet I preferred the softer, gentle side of me. Before we had begun this session, I shared this with the shaman. And here I was being asked to embrace that more vigorous side of me via the sword.

So, I brought up this very concern to Michael via the shaman. Michael responded that there was no way to wield the sword without being intense. He actually called it *ruthless compassion*. I can be gentle afterwards, he said. I must pick it up and be comfortable with my own intensity and trusting it! There is most absolutely compassion. But there has to be an edge to cut to what is true. Sometimes the sharper the sword the more compassionate it is, often with one swift movement of the sword. The intensity is actually the most loving thing I can provide, he stated.

He said that people know that he, Archangel Michael, can love and take the sword at the same time. *I save them years,* he said. As I recall these words, they speak as penetratingly as they did on this day. With these four words, everything made immediate sense. I have always been a "nip it in the bud" type person, confronting issues head on, not allowing them to fester, yet with very deep compassion and sensitivity, as well. It was profoundly clear that I needed to reframe my understanding of what the sword is truly about.

Here I was, a representative of Archangel Michael since 2001, and yet I had been ignoring the power of his sword all of these years. But it was also perfect timing. It was all by perfect design that I now align more closely to Michael in this way, like never before.

All this talk about the sword made me think of when I was dealing with the dark energies in earlier months. I was told by Michael, as well as a very close guide, that a battle of Light vs. dark was literally taking place right above me. That opened my eyes to the intensity of what is really going on in the bigger picture, not just in the physical but in the "ethers," as well. I needed to better understand the darkness and all while detached and staying out of fear, as fear only feeds dark energies.

As we know, fear is absolutely crippling. And yes, the energy of fear is literally the food of the dark. This is why fear mongering is at an all-time high now, as the dark is more intensely advancing their agenda. We can be aware, and then flick away the undesirable—flick, flick, flick—while always using the sword when necessary.

I am Michael's student and you may very well be too, and why you were led to this book. I was told I need to bring Michael's energy into the world in this way. The shaman said I will get more skillful with sword play. She said that the sword can cut to the truth, and when connected to truth and Light, I can trust it. This was exciting information—to have access to a Divine tool that will bring forward truth! She said I am so clear and Michael knows and trusts that I would never use it to harm.

The next question I asked was what exactly do I do with the sword. The shaman said that Michael just wants me to pick it up! So that's what I did in the following days, again and again. Every time I picked up the sword, I took the imaginary handle into my hand's grip, held the sword upright while placing the handle right at my third eye! I did this as if it was the most natural thing in the world, without even thinking about it, as if I've done this many times before. I imagined what the sword looked like and waited for more information to come forth as my training was just beginning. And it came forth effortlessly—not only through Michael, but also through many messengers and synchronicities over the next few months, and most powerfully during my pilgrimage to Canada.

Six weeks later, I shared with my cherished friend Mia via a Skype call the message from the shaman, and told her that she too may need to use the sword. Something that happened six years prior came to the forefront of her mind. She immediately looked up in her journal a post describing a time that Archangel Michael appeared to her. She was in an argument with someone and Michael, in the ethereal, handed her his sword for protection. I was even more stunned when she messaged me the image she drew right after this happened. As you can see below, it is a drawing of Mia *with the handle of the sword placed at her third eye!*

Needless to say, this was no coincidence. How amazing was it that Mia was given this same invitation directly from Michael years before, and yet we never had this discussion in the many years of our friendship until the most perfect time? And here she created this drawing of it so she would not forget, and yet to be seen by me when it would have the most profound impact. But what's absolutely extraordinary to me was that Mia saw the sword in the same position as I was now holding it, naturally.

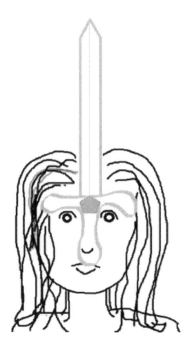

The actual drawing Mia created six years ago

You can imagine the effect this synchronicity had on me. This was Divine information flowing forth, and I would continue to receive validation upon validation of just how real and vital the understanding and usage of the sword would become. It was destined that these messengers and synchronicities would all magically come forth during these unprecedented times on our planet. The time is clearly... now.

In June, a couple of months *prior* to this meeting with the shaman, I was visiting in Sedona, Arizona. When walking in front of Cathedral Rock at Red Rock Crossing, Michael came through with a strong message. He said I must go to Lake Louise in Alberta, Canada. I had cancelled my plans to visit this year and was sad about it, but he insisted that I must not cancel. I have never not followed Michael's direct requests and I was not about to now.

After receiving his message, I turned around retracing the narrow path and was shocked to see a bright red feather on the ground, right where I had walked. It surely wasn't there moments before and it was clear that Michael put it there for me. On that very day, just prior to leaving for this walk, I had seen a picture of a feather my friend Kellee found at her doorstep, along with a chart of different colored bird feathers, what their spiritual meaning implied, and how they are strong signs from the angelic realm.

I could not recall ever coming across bright colored feathers like those shown in the chart and it made me strongly desire to. And then hours later, I happen upon a most beautiful, bright red cardinal feather. Also, both me and my friend Jeni had auspiciously seen a cardinal flying in front of each our cars on this very day, before this happened, and on opposite ends of the country.

When I walked a bit further on the path, I encountered a group of three and strongly felt to share the feather with them. The woman was very excited about it and even requested to take a picture of it. I asked where they are from. "Canada" they replied. Well of course they are from Canada! Michael wanted to be sure I heard him clearly. And I recently put it together that, of course, red (and white) is one of the two colors representing this country, and yet more symbolism was reflected from this feather.

The woman stated that the feather might be a sign or message, for instance that I would meet with a friend I didn't expect to or something like that. What a random point to make, but I made a mental note of it, as randomness from others often proves very telling; if not immediately, at some future point in time. She had no idea I was obsessed with signs and even wrote a book about synchronicity, but, of course, I then shared that nugget.

What is most extraordinary is that this woman prophesized, surely with help from Michael, just what would transpire. Or perhaps they appeared from another dimension simply to give me the necessary foresight—not the first time I've witnessed this. Because months later, it all unfolded effortlessly, as I did meet with a friend I didn't expect to and while in Canada, and her blessed presence was clearly guided by Michael—guidance we were both fully aware of. And here, when I received his message when in Sedona that I must go to Canada, I had no idea that his sword was to be a huge part of my future—I was fully unaware of the unfolding plan. And all while Michael was planting some big seeds, I'd soon find out.

Note: After editing this portion of the book about the red feather and Michael's call to visit Canada, I referred to a personal channel from Michael. I then looked up and saw a red-tailed hawk flying just outside my window. Where I'm living temporarily, in the suburbs, this is the first hawk I've seen in this subdivision. I then went to Facebook and at the top of the feed is an image of a sword in the stone and refers to

Merlin. Much more about Merlin later, but just to share how validating the signs continue to be.

A couple of months after Michael guided me to go to Canada, I began to plan the trip. He said that I must stay in the energy of that area, right in the hamlet of Lake Louise. I wondered how I would afford it. My savings was dwindling, I wasn't careful with money, and barely had income at the time. So, I needed cheap lodging. The famous Fairmont Chateau located at the head of Lake Louise costs $600-700 per night! Michael asked me to *just put it out there.*

So, I posted on my Facebook wall my need to stay at Lake Louise cheaply, and tagged several Canadian friends. One of them told me about a hostel at Lake Louise, and another told me about one in Banff, and I soon found that I could stay right near the lake, right in the village, for only $26 a night! I was blown away by this opportunity. And I proceeded to make reservations at four different hostels during the length of my trip to Canada.

Because Lake Louise and Banff areas are filled with tourists in the summer, I felt I must go in early October to avoid the crowds. Michael suggested I plan for late September through early October, and then it hit me. I would be there for his Feast Day on September 29th! So I centered the whole trip around this Divine day of Michael's. While our Archangels have no egos, and do not desire our praise and worshipping, I wanted to honor Michael in this way.

I would drive from Colorado and on the way to the Canadian Rockies, my plan was to first meet with some friends who live just outside of Calgary,

Alberta. When I contacted Rhonda, she gave me her address and invited me to stop by, but I felt so strongly that we needed to meet at the lake. Rhonda is an extremely busy entrepreneur running three companies with her husband, both compassionate stewards of Mother Earth, and I didn't know how she'd have time. However, the feeling that Michael wanted both of us to be there was unshakable.

Rhonda wrote "I definitely need to get back to Lake Louise soon—so many downloads there! Such a magical place!" She then mentioned Archangel Michael. Rhonda was surely hearing Michael's and my thoughts because without my saying anything, she suddenly and spontaneously decided that she would stay at the hostel with me for two nights, immediately booking them! I did not expect that at all, while immediately adoring her can-do attitude.

What further amazed me was when Rhonda added that she hasn't taken a break from her work in three years! I was so honored and very excited to meet with her. It eventually dawned on me that this was the prophetic message that Michael sent me through that Canadian woman in front of Cathedral Rock, that I would meet with a friend I didn't expect to! I didn't know Rhonda that well, and yet felt undeniably compelled to contact her... incredible. Everything was falling into place with remarkable ease and much excitement.

Prior to departing, I met with my beautiful friend Jeannie, a most gifted Angel Channeler, for a long overdue lunch. After telling her about all that was taking place, she felt that Michael had much more he wanted to say and through her, and that we needed to have a channeling session soon and before

I left. What I didn't know then was that Jeannie was about to become a most significant and validating part of this book and mission. In this session on September 21, 2017, Michael came through at once and everything resonated so strongly.

*The words for the day are, you are ready. You've been through trials and preparations for what is to come. So, this journey you are about to take is one that will bring you clarity and events and circumstances to get your work out more clearly. I need to tell you that you have proved that you are willing to do whatever it is. That you won't give up your work for abundance. This truly is a blessing to me, as well as to you.*

*You've trusted fully in me, in God, and put one foot in front of the other, oftentimes not sure where you were going but trusted you would be led along the right path. And so it is now, this trip, this journey, for the first leg of this journey brings you full circle. When you come back, things will begin to open up as if by magic. And that, too, is something that you will be documenting or relaying in your writings.*

With resolve and confidence, I shared with Jeannie that I keep attributing the sword work to the lake and that when I arrive in that beautiful energy, I will understand my mission with the sword more clearly. Jeannie sensed the very same. I added that the influences were continuing to "mess" with me, sabotaging me, and Michael validated this.

*You are being "messed" with. It's as simple as that, you are. I am aware, but understand this. Strength comes, you've taken the first step and it's picking up the sword. But like anyone who draws the sword, there needs to be knowledge with it. When you feel yourself in need of picking it up, feel it. It isn't enough just to pick it up. But what you need to feel is the energy and power that runs through you. Understand? It isn't the sword that does the work. But it's you. It's the power. You are the power, not the sword. The sword is just an extension of that power. It is taking the power that you hold and channeling it out. This is what you need to learn.*

These words proved extremely valuable, as you can imagine. I hung onto every word that Michael shared about using the sword as I knew there was so much to learn. And yet, when I would hold the sword in my imagination, and even wield it, the feeling and movement felt completely natural as if I've done this many times as a force for the Light.

Jeannie then summed up Michael's direction: "I'm seeing you literally holding this sword and there's power in it, but not as much power as you... almost as if you aren't aware of the power you have and the power that's coming through you. You are the actual power, it isn't the sword itself. The sword is where it comes out of you. He's saying you have to draw the power, you draw it in from the crown through the body and into your hands and out. You need to feel that energy, Michael's energy, for it's swift, it's powerful, and it's always loving."

The fact is—and this is something I will be addressing more in greater detail—we all have the power, we are the power, and Michael is introducing the sword as an extension of our power and combined with his and the Light! This makes me think of J.K. Rowling's famous quote: "We do not need magic to change the world, we carry all the power we need inside ourselves already: we have the power to imagine better."

Michael continued through Jeannie: *So you need to practice. Perhaps when thinking of someone, you need to practice it, like anyone would if learning to use something. So practice it with people you know who hurt you, visualizing it, anyone you think of that perhaps have been negative, or brought negative, harmful things to you. Practice taking the sword and feel it running through you... for protection.* Right there, I knew that this would be a most empowering act—and it proved to be so with practice. But it was not to be used, and I had no desire to use it, on people and situations in the past that were no longer affecting me. Only was it to be used in situations where I needed protection in the present.

Inherently, I knew that the sword would not be directly aimed at anyone, but before me as I first worked on protection or between myself and any persons from whom protection was needed. This was a tool I could use to protect and to conserve my energy—keeping my energy space impenetrable to dark or unwanted energies, and thus preserve my field. I shared with Jeannie that I'm being interfered with while I'm in training on how to use the sword, and that I feel they attempt mind control. Jeannie said "Yes, oh yes. When they really dig in, that's exactly what it is."

I replied that I feel to hold it for protection, and just to preserve my energy. Jeannie responded: "Exactly. It's to preserve your energy. It's to protect the dark from infiltrating the Light in your energy space, in *your* energy space. Or someone else's on a larger scale." There have been so many uses I was experimenting with, as I told her, such as raising it to lessen the effects of recent hurricanes and fires, and also to bring forward truths regarding them.

We talked about the trip some more. Jeannie referred to Rhonda saying "Words of wisdom come from her. It's almost like she is a teacher. That's interesting because usually you're the teacher." I said I already felt that, and literally told Rhonda that I feel I had a lot to learn from her.

Jeannie continued: "This is coming at the perfect time. Because when you come back here, something comes up. Something you're going to do, something he's (Michael's) going to ask you to do and he's not ready to tell you yet. But there's something, and you need, you really need to be able to have it (the sword) so you can protect. I'm seeing you as this beacon, there's so much light. Whenever the dark see it, it's this big beacon, they hone in on it. Your work is so light-filled and so important to the world. So that's who they go after."

# CHAPTER TWO

# The Pilgrimage to Canada

I will share in this chapter the full story of my guided journey to Canada so that you understand how this work was birthed. The following clearly demonstrates what happens when we follow guidance from the highest of the high. This mission was unveiled with one surprise after another, filled with magical validations of this very work, in ways I don't think even my imagination could have conjured up. These validations are a vital part of this book, as Michael made sure that his unique call and messages are undeniable to both you and me.

You will also hear of ways that our angels can influence matter, such as Michael making that red feather appear, as well as the instances at Lake Louise which left me in awe. But I'm getting ahead of myself. As I write these words, I can feel my body literally vibrating as this is how excited I am to write out this whole story for you. Because I know that those this book is intended for will understand and be inspired just as I was. I also know you each have your own incredible stories. When we share them, we open up the possibilities for each other.

Not long before arriving at my first destination once in Canada, I *heard* to "Look up," somewhat behind me, while on the expressway. There was a clear "U" (or "you") in the sky, so I stopped to capture it. When I later showed this to my friend Sally, she saw the "U" with a sword underlining it. Regardless of how one sees it, this was certainly an unusual sighting within a fully cloud-covered sky.

Note: Whenever you see the word *heard* italicized throughout the book, that's my way of referring to a telepathic hearing of the Heavens. I channel Michael telepathically; I do not hear his voice as some channels do.

When arriving in Okotoks, Alberta for a visit, the magic was set into motion right away. The spirit of a woman named Lillian, whom I never met, came through so clearly saying that she was with me and supporting me. She is the aunt of Leigh, a person I love and am very close to on a soul level. I never met Lillian, also known as Lily, as she passed years ago and lived in Canada. However, I felt a growing connection to her simply because she was so important to Leigh. And here I was, only a couple of hours drive from where she lived on the earth plane.

Just then, I realized I needed to stop and get gas but my American credit card didn't work at the gas pump, so I went into the convenience store. The clerk was extremely attentive, strongly wishing to converse with me. We engaged in some brief, ordinary talk, but he suddenly switched gears and said something completely out of context. I listened intently, as that is often when messages come from "above," through unknowing messengers "below."

He said that when something really bad happens, say a volcanic eruption where one was very unexpected, something really wonderful can come out of it, such as new land and growth. With this being so completely out of context, I felt that he was a messenger telling me that from all my heartache and challenges in recent months, something beautiful would emerge from it. Often, a "stranger" delivers the perfect message to us.

I then felt drawn to this Greek restaurant, as my first restaurant stop in Canada, and initially ordered a cup of strong Greek coffee. It was a random thing to order, but a strong Mediterranean brew kept coming up for me, synchronistically. When the waiter accidentally spilled a bit of coffee onto the saucer when setting it in front of me, he proceeded to say he was sorry but then not really, because this is a sign of good luck! He said I should get a lottery ticket.

The irony of his words brought a huge smile across my face as I look back at this moment. In my first book, *I Can See Clearly Now*[2], I declare that when water (or any fluid) spills, it is a sign of abundance! I had never heard of that theory before—it is something I discovered and felt strongly about on my own—and many readers wrote me over the years that they too began to shift their reactions to liquid spills. And here I was the recipient of this very message at a key time in my life.

By the way, that night when having dinner with my friend Shelly, Lotto 649 came up in conversation and I later went to get what was a winning ticket. Okay, it was just a mere $5 winner, but everything was unfolding so symbolically. I was enjoying every meeting with all these Canadians—they are indeed very friendly people as their stereotype suggests.

One of my planned stops in this area was to view the geological landmark Okotoks Erratic. It's the largest known glacial erratic in the world—also known as "Big Rock." I enjoyed exploring this huge and mystical boulder formation sitting unexpectedly

[2] Soliel, Mary. *I Can See Clearly Now*. Lincoln: iUniverse, 2008.

so in very flat land, and a fair distance from the Canadian Rockies.

After my visit there, I drove around awhile but was surprisingly and yet clearly guided to return to the rock formation. As always, I listen to higher guidance, and upon arrival I took some more pictures of this fascinating formation. When I *heard* to "Look up" suddenly, I was stunned to see this display of clouds that revealed a being (well, several, when you really look) with a sword pointing down! The sword is in the upper left quadrant of the photo.

Those familiar with my work may know that I capture images of clouds on a regular basis that reveal Heaven's messages, and published a book celebrating the signs called *Look Up! See Heaven in the Clouds*[3]. So this sighting further validated my new mission with the sword! And it was just a small taste of the magic Michael had in store for me and, ultimately, you.

When leaving Big Rock, I came across a woman walking her dachshund. I clearly *heard* to ask her what the dog's name was. That was a random thing to ask but as always I trusted and blurted out "What a cute dog. What is its name?" "Lily" she said. I instantly knew that Lillian sent me this validation to prove that she was with me. Had I departed even a minute earlier, I would not have experienced this synchronicity at this most mystical setting.

I left Big Rock and ten minutes later arrived at my next destination, the home I was staying at that night. I wanted to quickly drop off my luggage and get ready to meet my friend for dinner. My timing was perfect. As I parked outside this home, I saw a young woman with her Chihuahua. If you read my book about synchronicity, you know that Chihuahuas have been highly powerful messengers in my life, which I explain in Chapter Seven.

As I approached them, I again *heard* to ask what this dog's name was. She replied "Her name is Lily." *Incredible!* Two "Lily"'s within ten minutes of each other! And here this Lily lives in the house I was staying in that night. It was a beautiful blessing that both awed and warmed my heart.

Once in my room, I called my kids to let them know I arrived in Canada safe and sound. I excitedly shared with my daughter my meeting of two dogs

---

[3] Soliel, Mary. *Look Up! See Heaven in the Clouds.* Boulder: Twelve Twelve Publishing, LLC, 2015.

named Lily, one after the other and very soon after hearing from Lillian. Karen was amazed as she immediately reminded me that two days before I left for Canada, the exact same thing happened. When at this event we attended together, I had asked the owner of this small dog what its name was, and it was "Lily." Oh goodness, that was right, and it made me immediately think of Lillian then, too!

Lillian's magical way of connecting to me while in Canada was so surprising that I hadn't yet put it together that this occurred, as well, just before I left. Asking of a dog's name truly isn't my usual question to dog owners. Lillian must have whispered to me to ask that question even that first time, without my realizing it was her. She clearly wanted to connect with me, somehow orchestrating all of this, and she has been communicating with me regularly ever since. How astronomical are the odds that the three dogs I asked of their name, within three days of each other (and two of those within ten minutes of each other) were all named Lily?

Note: When editing the previous paragraph, I *heard* to search the top 10 female dog names (via www.rover.com). For 2017, Lily is not on the list. Even regarding the #1 most common name, "Bella," meeting three dogs in succession named Bella would still prove to be uncanny odds.

Even though traveling alone, I became ever aware that I had an entourage from another plane joining me in addition to Michael, including this special soul Lillian who offered a magical and healing presence. I also felt my dear grandmother

Mary with me as well, my traveling partner in spirit, and my guiding light.

Before I go further, I wish to repeat the same words I expressed in my book *I Can See Clearly Now*, where I shared countless synchronicities that could spark skepticism: "Some of my stories may seem too unbelievable to be true. Believe me, I am well aware of how karma works, and I have opened my heart with only the purest of integrity here."

The next morning, on September 27th, I headed for Lake Louise with unrelenting anticipation, and with the magic already in full swing. Once arriving at the small village and then taking Lake Louise Drive to the famous lake itself, I could feel the high energy of this area in my heart. I felt emotional—a "good" emotional—and that feeling continued during my visit to this lake of extraordinary beauty.

However, the following morning when I went to Moraine Lake, I found that the energy was even more intense there. While Lake Louise is known as Archangel Michael's lake, I felt his presence even more so at the grandeur of Moraine Lake.

At one point, and as mentioned in the Introduction, as I meandered along the path at Moraine, I was awed by the perfect and luscious aquamarine reflection, as seen on the cover of this book. When I began taking several pictures of this diamond-shaped gem, a sudden awareness came over me in literally just seconds. I would write a new book about Michael's sword and this mystical capture would serve as the cover of the book.

I truly had no plans at all to write another book at this time, and yet I felt it to my core. There was an overwhelming awareness that this was the very reason Michael brought me to this lake! His message of our new mission together was unveiled at, as mentioned before, what I now call the "Diamond Vortex."

And do I dare call it the inspiration for my *"magnum opus?"* These are the words Michael is whispering to me now, as I write this, and I had to look it up to make sure I knew what it meant. I do believe all of my spiritual writings hold great significance, most especially those written with Michael. But yes, I do feel that even though I'm just starting to write this book, it will be my most important work. Michael simply wanted me to own the significance of this mission.

Note: Weeks after writing the previous paragraphs, I just now put together what I saw when leaving the Greek restaurant in Okotoks, just after the lucky sign of the Greek coffee spill. I had no reason to include this picture until I just had an epiphany now.

"Magnum" is a power word that my friend Mia and I have used over the past year. She starting using this word as a symbol when I gathered with her and her family in Florence, Italy a year ago. We posed for a picture in front of the Magnum emblems, as you can see below, each just naturally extending our arms and meeting fingertips to fingertips, creating this visual. You see only the letter "M," but it stands for "Magnum," in this case for the ice cream brand. Interestingly, both our names begin with the letter "M," but we didn't think of that at the time.

This storefront was directly across from the famous Duomo. You can even see the cathedral's dome in the reflection on the glass. The fact that our fingers met perfectly centered below the dome's reflection was fully unplanned and unknown at the time, but in that moment, I fully recall that the pose itself felt guided. You could say our arms are like two swords meeting! There was something profound to all of this, and Mia gave honor to it when she immediately began using the word "Magnum," describing the power of who we are—specifically referring to our Divine Feminine power.

We have used this word as a noun in our communications such as "You are Magnum." Or as an adjective, as in "Have a Magnum day," for example. Perhaps "Magnum" is a word that needs further consideration. And Mia has a message for us to simply be Magnum.

As soon as I spotted the Magnum sign in Okotoks, I took a picture for Mia and messaged it to her. But here the meaning unveiled even further as I write this book. Michael just now helped me notice the "MAGNUM" logo *alongside this diamond graphic* as seen on page 31—and connecting it to his "magnum opus" reference regarding my book inspiration birthed at the Diamond Vortex!

Everything regarding this Diamond Vortex was magical. I found that as I first set my eyes on this eye-catching display, it just happened to be the most perfect timing as the reflection was best seen at this time of day, and on a very sunny day, at that. When

I walked by the same place a short time later, the reflection in these luscious blue waters was completely gone. Michael was orchestrating everything perfectly—with unmistakable clues and messages.

The magic multiplied when I returned to Lake Louise later that day. I kept feeling drawn to the area near where they rent canoes, and spent some time there. A couple asked me to take their picture and I sat down for a while. When I ventured toward the head of the lake right in front of the famous lodge, I was energetically struck by the appearance of someone who immediately resembled a dark influence that I had become increasingly aware of.

As soon as this man locked eyes with me and with an odd smile, I did an "about face" movement turning my back to him with an overwhelming uneasiness and realization that he was not of the Light. In that very same moment, I clutched my side and realized my purse was no longer with me (I wore it over the shoulder and neck). I could still feel the weight of it as if still wearing it, and yet it was not physically there!

Did I remove my purse just to take that picture? I highly doubted it but I returned to the bench I had just sat at and asked the few people now sitting there if they had seen a purse, but they had not. I suddenly felt this calm, this knowingness that Michael moved my purse! Yes, our angels and even passed loved ones can influence matter and this would not be the first time I've experienced this with Michael, but never before in this way.

The fact is I couldn't imagine leaving my purse in my car, especially when traveling outside the country with things like my passport, money, and credit cards in it, just sitting exposed on the floor of the car. I'm too careful to do that. And yet I felt sure it was there. I asked Michael if he removed my purse to scare me with my purse missing so that I would promptly leave the energy the man was emitting. He responded with a clear "Yes."

Sure enough, I returned to the car and there was my purse sitting on the car's floor. As I backed out my car, I was astonished by the personalized license plate on the car right next to me: "SKARGO"... I was "scared" about my purse which caused me to "go!" The plate was even surrounded by a "TESLA" plate cover, and Nicola Tesla is very special to my heart. To be clear, I did not fear the man at the lake, and I obviously had Archangel Michael's protection. But it was then that I was starting to feel as if I was living out my own version of *The Celestine Prophecy* story with a bit of *The Da Vinci Code* thrown in!

As I drove away, I realized I wanted a picture of this license plate to document this synchronicity, and thus circled around the parking lot. When I returned in that short period of time, there was now a white truck behind the car with the SKARGO plate, and with bright sunlight beams illuminating the cab of this truck. The license plate read 777! And it took up space in such a way I couldn't easily get around it, and thus got my full attention.

While I took pictures of this scene, I noticed that the truck was in the reverse gear and stayed that way. The auspiciousness of 777 and Divine Light protection was "backing into me." In the picture on the next page, you can see both of these vehicles and their license plates, while some distinguishing features have been erased.

All I could think of was the phrase that often comes to mind in one's consciously synchronistic life: "I just cannot make this stuff up!" The truck remained that way for some time and for an unknown reason, as the driver didn't seem to be waiting for a parking spot. After I took it all in and immortalized this moment with my phone's camera, I eventually squeezed my way around the truck. I will hold this memory in my heart because it exemplifies that when we choose to call forth and work with Michael, we are protected—he has our back! And this experience was a grand courage booster, to say the least.

When synchronicities like this line up in one's life, it is exhilarating and overwhelming to consider the enormous odds for such events to take place. We can easily dismiss it as chance. Or we can embrace and acknowledge the life-enhancing gifts bestowed on us when things like this occur. Divine synchronicity is a universal, unstoppable energetic force blessing all of us every single day. We need only notice the magic.

Michael explains this beautifully in *Michael's Clarion Call*:

*And speaking of coincidences, there are actually no coincidences, period. Some people don't want to believe that what is known as coincidence indeed carries meaning, often because it scares them. That makes the world too magical, and humans want to make sense of everything. And I say to you, get used to the magic. It's going to continue to increase. Synchronicities are on the rise. Miracles are on the rise. And when you desire and celebrate them, you attract more. This channel is, you might say, obsessed with them, and she also attracts splendid signs and what she considers to be magical moments every single day.* Nothing is too magical, in my view. Bring it on, Universe and angels!

My only sadness felt while at both Lake Louise and Moraine Lake were the extreme number of trees that seem to be dying or at least sick. It was distressing to see at least half of the trees affected, as well as I could guess. I still haven't found out the cause, but I have my theories. I wondered if other tourists were even noticing this.

I returned to the hostel after the purse scenario to rest up for the big day ahead—Archangel Michael's Feast Day. On September 29th, I arrived early at Lake Louise. After taking a walk and contemplating the day ahead, I created a video in honor of Archangel Michael, about connecting to the heart.

As described in my books with Michael, he teaches us that we are moving into a heart-centered way of living and being. I couldn't think of a way to better way honor him than to share this teaching. This is our future.

Michael teaches us that the heart has a wisdom greater than the mind and those of us seeking to grow our vibrations can and must learn to connect and communicate with it. He suggests that we literally place our hand (or hands) over our heart, close our eyes, and ask anything we wish. For instance, one could simply ask "What is it that my heart wishes for me to know now." And the answer will come forward, often in a combination of ways: perhaps through words, thoughts, feelings, sounds, and/or visions in our third eye, etc. These answers arrive instantaneously in a download of information, stimulating the senses *in literally just a second or seconds*.

While making this video, I held in my hand a special piece of labradorite that my daughter gave me just prior to leaving for Canada. When starting to work with the sword, I was wanting something to hold onto in the physical that had some weight to it, as it helped me to imagine and follow through with the sword work. As soon as she handed it to me, I knew this was its purpose. It was shaped as a long diamond, melding perfectly to my hand, and it even revealed a little heart shape in it. Interestingly, this mineral is used to help illuminate one's spiritual destiny and transformation, and aligns the body with higher energies. I brought it with me on the trip so I could work with it. As I walked away holding my tripod, the labradorite was missing.

I scoured the area where I created the video, but to no avail. I then recalled that I stopped for a moment at a different part of the grassy field to get a better handle on all I was carrying, and right there I saw a rock similarly shaped but larger. I picked it up and realized that Michael wanted me to have this rock too, which was energetically charged in this sacred area. It was shaped like a torch head and, again, melded perfectly to my grip. But where was my other rock? I somehow slightly grazed my hand across my stomach and realized that it was sitting in a little pouch in my sweater. I guarantee you that I did not put it there.

Prior to leaving for this trip, I had bought a new dark blue (representing Michael's color) top to keep me warm. It was the first day I wore it and I completely forgot there was a little pouch situated at my belly. Not only that, I would not have put a pointed rock there as it could have damaged my top or easily fallen onto my feet. I had no question that Michael put it there, again moving things, influencing matter which I imagined he can do especially easily in this high vibrational place where the veil is much thinner.

Next, I took both the piece of labradorite and the present from Michael to the lake and let the liquid crystal water charge up the precious rocks. When I stopped at the deli at the Fairmont Chateau to have lunch, I used my cell phone to visit Facebook, where I had posted my video honoring Michael, and was reading comments people left there.

My friend Bryan surprised me with the comment "Eyes out for the (dragon emoticon)s!" Underneath his words, he included an image of Archangel

Michael with his sword! It's as if Bryan somehow knew of what I experienced the day before, when Michael took my purse away to help me avoid negative energy from the being at the lake. Did he on some level know I was being warned and thus reminding me to keep my eyes open? It was quite a surprising and unexpected comment and image to receive on this day, under my video post—so I knew I needed to explore further.

I messaged Bryan right then: "What made you say that? You are right! Please let me know, I will write later." He responded "Well, I was in Espanola, NM all last week and the B&B I stayed in had saint-themed rooms, and I was in Michael's room." The image above was over the bed. I responded "Wow!

But what made you say to basically watch out for the dark in this case, on this day?"

Bryan replied, "Haha, that would be a long one to unpack. Maybe I feel like Michael is wading through some heavy darkness right now. But I think of dragons as shadow energy with the potential for powerful transmutation, not just annihilation. Actually, wouldn't it be beautiful to see one reflected in the glassy surface of that incredible lake?"

And right there, in Bryan's response, netted out once again my new work and possibly your work too, dear reader—to help Michael, as Lightbearing humans on this earth plane, address and transmute the darkness. Bryan had no previous knowledge of my introduction to the sword. I did not mention the sword or anything connected to it in the video I created. How is that for validation through a fellow human being?

Indeed, I needed to keep my eyes out, and with Michael always by my side he protects me as he protects all of us who turn to him. Since my travels the year prior, I found that wherever there is great Light, in known spiritual places and vortices, it also attracts the dark.

Because of snow in the forecast, Rhonda and I delayed our meeting a few days. I went to Kelowna, British Columbia to escape the snow. When arriving there, I soon went to sit by Okanagan Lake.

At one point, Michael *whispered* to me to "Look up!" I had to arch my head way back to see the inverted cloud, pictured on the next page. Had I not *heard* him, this was far from my line of vision and I would not have seen it. The visual of this break in the clouds took my breath away. At first I saw a being with raised arms and wearing a wide skirt, as if dancing or in celebratory mode.

When I posted it on Facebook, a friend saw what I didn't see at first—a hand grabbing onto something! Natalie commented "Hand holding a rose. See the knuckles on top of the stem?" That further took my breath away. I then saw that it was indeed a hand. But I saw it as grabbing onto a sword's handle! Here was yet another sword message in the clouds. But the rose visual is beautiful and so appropriate too, since the rose is a symbol of the Divine Feminine, so perhaps it is both. Mia then chimed in with the comment "Holding the sword." Yes!

When it was time to return to Lake Louise, I couldn't get back to that energy and beauty soon enough. On the morning of October 4th, Rhonda texted me that she'd meet me at the hostel in a couple of hours. Two hours later, I had literally just backed my car into a parking space to wait for her and she pulled up right next to me, door to door, not even yet knowing it was me. We both knew that our synchronistic timing was previewing a synchronous and blessed visit together.

This was the first time we met in person. I really didn't know Rhonda that well, yet felt connected to her, a soul family member, and it was very clear to us both that Archangel Michael wanted us here together at his vortex. Rhonda is all about seeing things as they are, and naming it with great love and compassion toward all. She cuts right to the truth, as if she is already using the sword, and it was perfectly orchestrated that we join forces at Michael's lakes.

To this day, I feel that we both know that a lot more went on in the ethereal, as that is what happens especially when two or more gather for sacred reasons to help the Earth and the Heavens. But enough magic happened that we were indeed aware of, and with much joy and celebration.

It was when we went to Moraine Lake the next day that Michael really blessed us with a powerful message. When we arrived at the Diamond Vortex, I told Rhonda I felt this was the main place to be and we should just hang out here for a while. She fully agreed.

Rhonda being ever dynamic, warm, and out-going, whenever she saw tourists (which was near constantly), she'd offer to take their picture with their cameras. A group of four gathered near us, and I was vaguely aware that Rhonda offered to take their picture in front of the reflecting diamond sight.

When I looked up, I was awestruck. A young woman with the group was posing with a piece of wood that fully looked like a small sword in her hand. In fact, she held it as if ready to use it. She was clearly holding the sword as if in warrior mode! I took a picture of them to document not only more validation, but it occurring just where I received the inspiration to write this book about the sword!

I had this strong feeling I was supposed to have this wooden sword, as a symbol and remembrance. What was even more extraordinary was that as this person walked from the site of the picture taking, she left the sword standing against a rock right before me! I just stared at it, taking it all in. So, I now have this gift, and will always have it as a tangible reminder of my mission and the magic that continually revealed it. Did these people come from another dimension too, just to make this point?

When the group left, I exclaimed to Rhonda that I couldn't get over the sword symbolism. She said she had noticed that very piece of wood sitting there, looking like a sword. She literally wondered if I was supposed to have it, and it was just then that the young woman picked it up and posed with it as if it was indeed a sword. And then she left it for me. Michael surely put it there to begin with! I had told Rhonda the day before that I was wanting a sword, but was using the rocks as substitutes for a sword's handle. Now I had a sword! And it was a light one and easy to wield... perfect.

Photo by Rhonda Ann Clarke

Soon after, Rhonda took the wooden sword as well as a crystal her husband gave me and charged them up in Moraine Lake, just as I did with my rock "swords" days before. It was a sweet gesture. She then took a powerful picture of me with the sword against beautiful violet and magenta rays emitted from the sun (unfortunately you can't see the rays' colors in this black & white photo, but you can see it in color in my gallery at www.marysoliel.com). With many thanks to Rhonda, this served as beautifully relevant symbolism connecting the sword to the sun. Archangel Michael is known to be the Angel of the Sun. Michael gave me my last name "Soliel," also connecting me to the sun. (This story is described in my first two books). Thus, I especially treasure this photograph.

# CHAPTER THREE

# Processing the Sword's Power

Upon my return home from Canada, I spent the following week writing the previous two chapters while all was still fresh in my mind. I felt such urgency to get home and get to work on this book that I drove straight through—twenty-seven hours in the car with necessary stops and naps. On the way home, and each and every day since, I practiced working with the sword.

After a few days home, it was clear that I must schedule another session with Jeannie. Michael wanted some more information to come through her for the validation I requested—as I most certainly desired. Because of my experiences of dealing with dark energies, I was most concerned about putting this precious and powerful information about the sword out into the world. I wanted to be absolutely sure and without a doubt that I was taking all appropriate actions.

Of course, as Michael said in his introductory message: *There will be no power to the sword if used for dark purposes, if used to harm or influence others' lives or aspects of life that are not to be tampered with. My sword is to be used for only the highest of purposes, three purposes, and they are for Light, Truth, and Protection.*

Jeannie came through soon after my request with messages that gave me deep comfort and renewed excitement for this project. At this point, she was completely unaware of what occurred at Lake Louise, nor of Michael's messages about the sword. She started out with this message from Archangel Michael:

*Is there any doubt that you are to write this book? It was clear, as clear as I could make it and you hear. Our connect is powerful. Now understand this, your fear of people misusing the sword? It needs to be wrapped in Light and love for anyone to pick it up. If it's wrapped in Light and love it cannot harm. And so, this sword that I give you and all swords that come from me can be wrapped in Light and love, this is what I do. So, do you see, no one can pick up the sword to misuse it. As this book comes out, you constantly focus on the Light and love. And also in the book there should be a place where it clearly states that the sword will have no power... NONE... unless it's wrapped in Light and love. So those who take it and try to misuse it... they won't be able to.*

My human self was so grateful for the extra validation that basically mirrored what came through Michael in his message to me while in Kelowna. There will be no power to the sword if used for ill intent. And then came a deeper understanding of why I was being tampered with by those aligned with the dark.

*Understand, what has happened in the last year is because the dark understands. They see what is coming for you. Do you not know that they knew about this sword before you did? Just as the Light sees your path or everyone's path, so also does the dark. They have the same abilities. It is on this side of the veil, the dark hones in on those they see who are becoming powerful... whose work is to help the world, to help bring Light, to help raise the vibration. Theirs is the opposite. They know just as we do, they see the future or the potential.*

I was grateful for Michael's validation through Jeannie. They tried to get to me and stop me, before I got to this place of spreading more Light. The dark is "messing" with many true Lightworkers. And it is very important to be aware that many of the instigators are actually posing as "Lightworkers."

They—or the entities working through them *with or without their awareness*—use influential means to affect the person holding the Light which may include psychic attack, mind control, and attempts to confuse with outright deceptions. For those who are consistently feeling they are having thoughts that aren't their thoughts, the reaction is simple. If they are not your kind of thoughts, it is probably because they are not your thoughts. So, transmute these thoughts, say positive affirmations if you feel to, and most especially protect your field, as you will learn to how raise the sword with Michael. We must protect our beautiful minds in all ways now, and we have the power to do just this.

Scores upon scores of people are doing amazing things for this world, whether consciously working for the Light or not. We need to be aware of what is going on, though, with the small minority that is wreaking havoc, *knowingly and unknowingly*, so that we preserve our well-being—our hearts, souls, and minds. The use of our God-given intuition has never been more vital. We must grow this muscle now as we find its necessity rising.

Intuition can be triggered when a person comes on too strong, suddenly rushing into one's life with inauthenticity. When I recently met this man for the first time in person, who had clearly tried to hone in on me, I had a most unique headache for 24 hours. I rarely get headaches, and certainly never ones that last nearly that long. Another time, I had just met a woman who immediately and oddly wanted to perform a "healing" on me, which I allowed. It left me with a horrible headache, followed by much chaos in my life for several days. Yes, healings often cause symptoms to arise, sometimes even growing worse before getting better, but it was clearly not the case in this situation. Lesson was learned because the fact was I allowed this healing to take place, despite my reservations once it began.

Many have shared with me similar experiences. One friend, who provides channeled readings, called to check on me when I went through my challenging time this year. She said that many of her clients constantly tell her they feel they are being psychically attacked. Another friend told me she was being intensely psychically attacked, resulting in headaches, as well. She was having thoughts she felt were not hers and yet it was making her question so much in her life, including her new relationship with her boyfriend, when in reality all was well.

The dark utilizes a conquer and divide approach. If we are unhappy with relationship issues, especially, it can lessen our Light and our effectiveness in anchoring in Light for the planet. Fortunately, this woman was highly aware, got in touch with her true feelings, while reasoning out what was really going on.

Here is a message from Michael on March 26, 2017 that addresses this topic:

*I believe that many of you would agree that life feels so different now. At times, you feel you need to place a new anchor somewhere but you don't know where to do so. I ask you to drop your anchor in our hands, those of us from the Heavens who are committed to your individual missions and lives. Drop your anchor and know that we see all and we will protect you, so feel the depth of that feeling of safety.*

*This channel hesitates for me to talk about this as she is always seeking the positive view of things but the fact is she has experienced some attacks from influences that are not of the Light. She retains her strength because she is constantly anchoring with us, constantly in connection with us. She has never experienced anything like this before and yet I will speak for her and tell you, she is aware of the battles going on between the Light and dark. Even right 'above' her. And she has our full protection.*

*And so, I tell you the same. Anchor with us, expect and recognize that you are indeed protected. Do not let anyone take away your Light as these are only "games" that you must not give your attention to... to the best of your ability. Call on us and know that we are here for you, loving you, appreciating you, supporting you, and protecting you.*

I posted this message to my Facebook wall which resonated with many, adding the comment: "I like that Michael is naming it as games, as that is how I see them now. Only giving enough attention for understanding to those working hard for the Light and feeling 'messed' with. Several have told or written to me of similar experiences, so, obviously, Michael wanted to address this through me. The Light is Winning. Love Always Wins."

What was especially striking was that just a few hours before Michael's message came through, I took a walk and came upon this extraordinary rock, as seen pictured on the next page. This bulky and unearthly rock was seemingly placed right in the middle of the dirt road for me. Do you see half way down this rock the defined eye on the right and the blackened, masked eye to the left? What you can't see in this black and white photo is the extraordinary, multi-colored crown above the face.

There was one person who instantly came to mind when I saw this face on the rock. How ironic is it that just hours later this young man messaged me with a comment regarding the post, a comment I questioned the genuineness of? This was the first time he had ever directed a message to me on Facebook. And it was in relation to this very message from Michael, about attacks from the dark. It was time to address the clues that were coming forth in perfect timing, and in the most unexpected ways. I needed to look beyond the surface of how things would appear to most, and rather pay attention to Michael, along with my intuition.

Almost six months later, Michael whispered loudly and suddenly, when I was in a public setting, telling me to put up protection "Now!" Seconds later this very man was in front of me. My concerns and skeptical feelings appeared to be for good reason. He and his companion were very cold to me. And even though he knew me, he acted as if he did not. He proceeded to circle around me looking at items in a store. I strongly knew, instinctually, that something was up with his circling around me, and yet I also knew I had Archangel Michael's protection.

How could I doubt my concerns when I heard Michael's warning just seconds before? Never before has Michael warned me like that! Minutes later in another part of the store, I saw him full of life and laughing heartily, an extreme and rapid change in disposition. I then caught him staring deeply at me from a distance. With Michael clearly overseeing the situation, I held no fear and yet was keenly aware.

Now this is the very being I thought of when I saw that man standing at the front of Lake Louise, when Michael made my purse disappear. It wasn't him as a physical being, but it perfectly represented him, as if he teleported into this body—as odd as that sounds. When our eyes locked and I felt immediate discomfort, I saw these same eyes. But again, I was shown that I was clearly protected and thus held no fear. Everything was coming together, especially my deeper understanding of what was occurring behind the scenes. But I also know there is still much I do not understand.

Just now, as I write this, I asked Michael about the looping or circling. In recent years, I have found myself naturally doing this either when walking grounds in areas that need healing or even accidentally making wrong turns (but on some level, not wrong) while driving and looping in areas that needed the same. When performing healing work in

Europe, I especially found myself naturally looping, while making healing intentions. But I ask you now, Michael, when he circled me, is that especially why I felt you wanted me to put up protection?

*This soul has a very dark side. He is not as he appears. You did not want to see it as you want to see the Light in everyone. It's not just a shadow, he carries dark intentions. You were being targeted, it was planned, and you heard my whispers for protection. I wanted you to be consciously aware but while staying out of fear. He is extremely gifted and sought to use those gifts in a way that is not of the Light. You protected yourself, but his circling was used to "mark you," to intend to affect your light. When you loop or circle, it is a power movement and symbol to amplify your Light and your intentions. But this same practice can be used for dark intentions amplifying the negative, as well.*

Michael's message made me think of my friend John who not only introduced me to this young man's work but I recently sensed that John was also being unknowingly "marked," and with telepathic interference, not necessarily by this same person, but specifically by people in this person's "group."

Ever since John began to work with them, work he said I was supposed to be a part of but I immediately knew to decline—the relationships in our circle drastically and dramatically changed. His first request to have me join the group didn't even reach me; by no coincidence it was "intercepted" as I was clearly not to engage in this manner. I recently recalled when Michael once warned me to physically leave the room when these same people were about to speak at an event. Despite really enjoying the company I was with, I listened to Michael and left. It is extremely rare that he gives me warnings such as this. It took me months to put all of this together, and I know it's just a part of a complex situation.

While pondering these thoughts, I just now went to Facebook and saw at the very top of the feed a post from John promoting the leader's upcoming event! I gasped at the synchronicity, on top of the fact that I very rarely see John's posts in my feed. It was Divine timing and more validation from Archangel Michael.

Earlier this year, when a completely separate and much more distressing situation exploded with different, and yet somewhat connected players, I found myself thrust onto a huge learning path ultimately leading me to prepare for my new mission and write this book. I kept my experiences under wraps. Only Michael knows the full story of what occurred with me, and it will stay that way—I will not give names or specific details to anyone and do not want to give it energy. Nor do I wish to bring up fear in others, but only enough information for awareness, to help prevent situations in their own lives. If we aren't aware and we do not follow our intuition, we can experience major setbacks. I learned this lesson very well. Deep suffering is not fun, but it is an excellent teacher.

With this very rock placed for me on the dirt road at the most perfect time, I embraced with much gratitude to Michael the clues he has and continues to leave me, often very extravagant clues. I keep this extraordinary rock as a perpetual reminder that all will be revealed. With our free will to request Archangel Michael's protection, we can remain vigilant and under Michael's watchful eyes which can see everything. It is essential to keep in mind that he can see what we cannot.

The masks we all wear are dissolving. And at the very core of all of us is only love. Michael said in *Michael's Clarion Call*:

*People just take love energy and distort, manipulate, redefine, and change the energy to something that no longer looks like love, until you unravel it to find its true essence. So that means if you hate thy neighbor, but then release the arguments, the words, the misunderstandings, the anger, the misbehavior, and look at him, you see that at his core essence is love. If you hate another, but then start to see they come from God as you do, well that does not mean that you have to join them for tea; but you can forgive and let go, and take notice of the love at their very core. The world isn't as scary a place when you see that at its core all comes from love.*

As a wise and dear friend wrote me following my trip to Canada: "Concepts like evil and the dark side inject fear and duality into our experience of truth. It's our job to protect our minds lest we join the dual perspective. Your (Michael's) sword is a means to maintain your life in truth."

I've avoided concepts of evil and the dark side throughout my whole life. However, we must find a way to acknowledge the darkness without allowing the injection of fear and duality as my friend pointed out—we have control over how we react to it all. These words *protect our minds* are most wise and vital to heed, especially now.

The extreme dark has affected the natural balance of duality, immensely so—causing Michael to sound his new and urgent call. We must have the necessary awareness while also maintaining our high vibrational ways of living and being as we experience life amidst the duality. Clearly, we have a fine line to walk, but a necessary one. Our angels can and are helping us through. And now we have Michael's sword to empower us like never before.

This book has taken me well out of my comfort zone, yet oftentimes going out on that limb is just where we need to go to make real change happen. Michael has proven it to me again and again how important it is to discuss the full picture. I really do not enjoy discussing the negative and dark aspects of life that I've shared here. Those who know me personally know me to be very positive, an eternal optimist who is always focused on the Light. However, the only way forward at this point, for us all, is to bravely acknowledge and transmute the darkness that is absolutely a part of our lives on this Earth—darkness that has gotten way out of hand—and this includes the shadows within each of us, personally, as we transmute them as well!

Jeannie and I met for lunch on October 18, two days after the reading following my trip to Canada. She said that while we spoke to each other, so much more was wanting to come through from Michael so we should gather again for another session. But some things couldn't wait, including this powerful point Michael wanted to make when discussing the sword, and she let me record her messages.

Michael said: *Do not intend to use the sword to destroy but to protect and to ward off. This is what I do many, many, many times every day, every second, I protect those of the Light, I protect my children. So, this is a gift to those of the Light who wish to use it. I'm offering this now to your world but it must never be used in vengeance. But for love and for protection, not in vengeance. The sword may be used to "destroy" or cast out, not with hatred but in protection.*

Note: The word "destroy" is set in quotation marks for an important reason. We know that energy, nor a dark spirit, can be destroyed; it can ideally be transmuted, but at least cast out. Michael clarified: *Your world may understand "destroy" but perhaps you may want to clarify or use the term "cast out" or "cast away" or use the following explanation for they are spirits, understand. And spirit can't be destroyed.*

*In war, and this is truly coming to pass in your world. It's what we all see even those, the beings from other stars and planets recognize, what is coming to the Earth. The light and the dark in a battle. There will be a time that the casting out of those dark and evil beings will be necessary. But to help you understand it a bit better, look at Satan. He was never able to be destroyed, simply cast out of the light, so it is with these demons and evil beings. They are cast out.*

*The sword can be used to protect and cast out if the circumstances warrant it. Keep it at neutral and with love but there is going to come a time that we are literally going to have to fight.* "That's why he wanted me to watch *Joan of Arc* a couple years ago," I responded. *Correct,* he says. Jeannie added that "We're such light beings but sometimes you can't just stand back and be complacent. You have to get up and you have to take up the sword."

Lightbearers resonating to this are being called into modern day Joan of Arc roles as we embrace our Divine Feminine power and this includes men—let me be clear! The Divine Feminine is rising in all of us—the sacred Masculine and Feminine. I know these words are very unsettling, especially the words about war and dark beings. They were to me, and yet I was grateful as I always am for the truth— and especially for the protection, for all of us.

Mary: My question is what exactly can it cast out, even though we are using it with no vengeance, but for protection and with love.

*As the dark gets stronger, dark entities and even demons are becoming more apparent in your world. This is what it can cast out. So you see, it isn't the human, but it is the darkness in them—that entity or that demon.*

Jeannie: In other words, if it's a person, someone who is really dark, it pushes that entity out of the being who they are using. It cannot kill it, but it pushes it away.

Michael continued through Jeannie: *We have always said you are a teacher, you speak eloquently, you share what comes directly from me, you are representing me in your world. You speak for me, you act for me, you write for me. This is why I have such great respect, you were chosen long before you came to this Earth and so it is. I am grateful because even though this was your choice, living on Earth has its challenges and you could have easily made another choice saying this is too difficult, I choose not to do this, but instead you stand up. You stand for me, you stand for God, you stand for Love, you stand for*

*Light. You teach it. You write it. This is your work. It is your work.*

Michael *heard* my question about protecting *his* children, as he never called us his children before in my communications with him.

Jeannie explained what she was hearing: "We are all God's children but Michael's children, that's a little bit different. There is a connect, so yes, he will step in and help when anyone, anytime, specifically asks for his help. There is a connect between certain people and him. Just as with each Archangel, the work is connected to various people. Yes, so he'll work with them more." Michael added: *I love all and everyone is God's children, but we are not God.*

Michael's point is that he loves all people and helps every single soul that asks for his help. We all have free will and the angelic realm cannot interfere unless we ask. We are each assigned to an Archangel. For instance, I know of healers who mostly work with Archangel Raphael. To be clear, *the invitation to use Michael's sword is open to all true Lightworkers*, no matter their affiliation with a particular Archangel.

Michael then delivered a potent warning to those who attempt to use his sword, yet not in the name of Love, but rather to harm:

*If one does use it for vengeance, it comes back tenfold to them, if that's their intent. It cannot work, but if they try, all that negative energy comes back tenfold. The sword has no power, it will be powerless, however it is the intent to use it for that. The intent itself will come back to them tenfold.*

It wasn't until November 13th that I had another reading with Jeannie, and it was a profound one. I wanted to delve further into what Michael touched on during lunch a month prior, and he came through immediately:

*There is a sense of urgency. Your world is in crisis. And it is getting worse. The time is now. Now.*

Mary: Michael, when you said *keep it at neutral and with love but there is going to come a time that we are literally going to have to fight,* can you elaborate some more? Does that mean we are going into war in the physical, or battles we each have personally?

Jeannie: He says both.

*It is both. There is the war of Light and dark as you are already aware of. So those who are of the Light will be battling on both fronts, literally for the Light, for their right to continue on the Earth. So, there will be war on the Earth in the physical as well as in the spiritual.*

Again, this was not news that any of us wish to hear. There have always been senseless wars on Earth and, apparently, we aren't quite done with these barbaric expressions on this beautiful planet. Not only do we as individuals build karma, but regions and countries do, too. So, for those countries that bully other countries, commit unnecessary attacks, wars, and more, it would make sense by Universal law that the pendulum swings back.

I explained to Jeannie that I understood from Michael that we couldn't work with Michael's sword effectively until now. With more people waking up during these chaotic times, the sword work will be much more effective now.

*There, you see. You just spoke of your work, don't you see? This is the purpose of the books, all of them, and especially this one. This is your work, it's waking people up. You're creating an army now, so to speak. An army of Lightworkers. This is essential to the very survival of your planet. The sense of urgency is there as we see the dark stepping up. It's evident in every part of your world. There isn't anywhere that isn't affected. So, this, this is your work.*

*The sword is given to you so that you can teach others how to use it and use it properly. You've been getting instructions downloaded and you are aware of that.*

Mary: Yes. You say to keep emotion out of it. You also said to keep it at neutral. So, when you raise the sword, you are just channeling out this energy, and that energy is taking care of it. With intensity, but not emotion.

*And that is correct. Intensity is... what is it? It is focus. They are and can be one and the same. So, you use it with focus. Intend on using it for the good, for the Light, and only for the good and the Light.*

Mary: I have been practicing this every day. I'm not seeing things shift as much as I thought I would. But I'm in training, so that I can write this book, and I'm modifying things as I go along. But the power isn't coming through yet fully. I feel I'm not ready.

*It's more about aligning yourself and staying in that neutral place. It's difficult for you as with anyone to really be in a neutral position when you see what is going on in the physical world and in your immediate world. Staying neutral, staying neutral, staying neutral. And not letting the emotions come in. You're correct. You are practicing now. You are practicing with those who already have intended to harm or impede your progress of the Light. This started, do you see, when you were in Sedona and New Mexico. Now more than learning to use the sword, for you are already adept at that part, but it is staying in the neutral place.*

Mary: That's exactly what I'm feeling because I catch myself and say "No, be neutral." It's a very fine line to be both neutral and yet intense, focused. And then the power will come through fully, right?

Jeannie: Correct! And then it will come in. You'll feel it. You'll literally feel it, running right down your arms from the crown straight down your arms and hands. You know the story you read about Merlin.

Mary: Yes, my daughter just told me this story!

Jeannie: When he pulled the sword and how he felt the power, a sting down his arms. That's how it's going to be for you.

Mary: And everyone who is meant to use it!
Jeannie: Yes!

Mary: Here is something I have always wanted to understand. Even great people who hold great Light experience difficult and even intense karmic retribution for their less than desirable actions, often immediately. The extreme dark influences are doing horrific, horrific things, killing people really, and where is the karma?

*Let me try to help you understand. Satan or the devil or whatever you choose to use as a term was an angel and yet still he turned towards the dark, cast out. If it can happen to an angelic being do you not think how much easier it is to happen to a physical being in your world?*

Mary: But it's almost like they get some free ride with karma.

*But being in the dark is their karma. There is no joy in it, ever. Only pain, only anger, a tortured soul, so to speak. Would you not consider that payment?*

Michael's words had quite effect on us both. I feel there is much more to be understood on this subject, but for another time. Many years ago, before I knew what karma was, someone close to me asked why someone at his work kept getting away with such horrible acts onto others. I responded that he doesn't know what is going on in this person's private life, and that he cannot possibly see everything. I had the answer already within me decades prior. We simply cannot see everything.

Note: Just minutes after editing these last few pages in early December, I was once again struggling with all the talk about darkness as it's very difficult for me to address it here, as much as I know I must. So, I took a short break and Michael immediately gave me the strength and courage I needed in a most unexpected way. I visited Facebook, and at the top of the feed was a post of a Ted Talk on "The psychology of evil," given by psychologist Philip Zimbardo. Yet again, this was no coincidence and was perfectly and synchronistically relevant. While not my favorite topic, I knew I must listen to this talk.

As the YouTube.com description of this February 2008 talk stated, this lecturer "knows how easy it is for nice people to turn bad. In this talk, he shares insights and graphic unseen photos from the Abu Ghraib trials. Then he talks about the flip side: how easy it is to be a hero, and how we can rise to the challenge."

"God's favorite angel was Lucifer," explained Philip. "Apparently, Lucifer means 'the light.' It also means 'the morning star' in some scripture. And apparently, he disobeyed God and that is the ultimate disobedience to authority. And when he did, Michael the Archangel was sent to kick him out of Heaven, along with the other fallen angels." How incredible the timing of finding this video, even noting our Archangel!

As he says half way through the talk: "So Milgram is quantifying evil as the willingness of people to blindly obey authority..." The compelling validations continue to illuminate our need to avoid complacency and rather wake up and follow *our own drummer*, no longer influenced by "authority," the dark authority.

The ultimate purpose of this talk was summed up at the end: "Let's oppose the power of evil systems at home and abroad. And let's focus on the positive. Advocate for respect of personal dignity, for justice and peace, which sadly our administration has not been doing." We have to be aware and stay out of fear, and put our focus on the Light into action.

We can change not only the past and the present, but *we can also shift the potentials of the future.* May we keep this strongly in mind that even with prophecies that we don't want to come to pass, we can change what is prophesized to come—may we use the sword in this way. And with that, let's now learn about Michael's New Call.

# CHAPTER FOUR

## Michael's New Call

*D* *ear agents of change, every single one of you. I*
*wish for you to listen closely, and, perhaps,*
*read these words a few times to really take them in.*

*I AM Archangel Michael sounding a new call,*
*and it is to step into a whole new paradigm and way*
*of being through your every day. This way requires*
*action on your part. A free will planet limits the*
*effect of what the Heavens can do to create change.*
*And so I am calling on those of you whose hearts*

*hear me, to step up your commitment of bringing Light forth onto your beautiful but ailing planet.*

*Do you see that with your intention to be an active force of Light, to carry my sword into your daily life, you will create change that cannot happen without you? Does this sound too grandiose or too much to take in? Do you feel up to heeding this call? I tell you that there is no greater or more significant work you can do for yourself, your fellow beings, or the Earth than to carry and raise my sword at this time. For the time is ripe for this work and it will illuminate your Earth. It will bring forth Light, truth, and protection into the darkest recesses of your inner and outer lives. This isn't just affecting life now, but the past and distant past, and most certainly your future as you create Heaven on Earth.*

*Think of it this way, exercising your free will to use my sword and spread Light, truth, and protection will finally help free humanity. As the Light illuminates the dark, the dark will no longer have this atrocious grip it has had on all of life. I will be working with each of you as a team, as you channel the power of the Light through you, your body, and out the sword. This is what I do all the time, but only in instances where I can interfere.*

Note: I came across a mini-reading that my friend Mia provided for me on March 27, 2017 that relates to this.

Mia talked about a pain I was carrying and its origin was not of this time. She wrote: "it goes back, back in a time where wars (I am sorry, I needed to use this exact word) were present in almost every area of our Planet

Earth. I feel Archangel Michael wants you to know it is him speaking... It's a concept hard for a human mind (in this stage of evolution) to understand; it is about you, you as an 'archetype' of the Light working its way through the density of the 'duality' and it is affecting all the timelines, all the 'times' and 'spaces.'"

Interesting to note, Mia received this message well before we knew about the new work with the sword. And her message fully relates to Michael's message that opens this chapter, and how this work will affect all time and space. More seeds of Michael's new call were being planted, and through Mia yet again.

Michael came through with several messages for you and me in late 2017. Throughout this chapter, I include the actual dates his messages were channeled, along with various journal type entries of relevant and related occurrences. Following a deeper explanation of Michael's call, you will then be invited to work with his sword.

I feel it is important to share at this point that over the years, I am not constantly channeling Michael for information and understanding. In large part, he has wanted me to learn on my own, through my personal experiences and certainly through synchronistic guidance. Sharing growth and wisdom achieved via personal experience and coming from the same perspective as everyone else, yet overseen by his guidance and support, of course, has been a most effective way to spread his messages. I hope you see this, by this book's example.

My life is filled with joys, challenges, successes, failures, happy surprises, heartaches, as well as a healthy dose of awe-inspiring magic and miracles that lift me on a daily basis. When I need Michael's help, when I desire clarity about something, of course I go right to him—and we all have this same right and ability! Whenever he has a message for me or the masses, I feel it straightaway and receive each message. But mostly, I am just being, observing, and acting on what my heart tells me to.

My heart told me to post this picture as my Facebook profile picture. I had never seen it before and yet it surfaced at the perfect time, just a week before I left for Canada. This symbolized Michael's call so perfectly.

Source: "We Are Human Angels" Facebook Page

I did not understand the sword in just one sitting. It has taken time and experience to deepen my understanding. The way Michael teaches is by coming through at different angles so that you really understand what he is saying and through multiple and deepening messages—I love his way. These messages may appear repetitive at times, but they are actually validating and providing an increasingly richer and deeper perspective.

Seven years ago, I questioned how I could put my first channeled book *Michael's Clarion Call* out into the world when there was so much new information I never heard of before. I was concerned about how it would be received. Even though I fully trusted Michael's information, there was also this need for validation to gain the courage necessary. I eventually addressed my discomfort by going through my whole manuscript and highlighting in color all the passages that were "out there," things that I never heard before. Synchronicity and other messengers validated every single one and I ended up including everything in the book. And so much he spoke of years ago is occurring now in our reality.

When I pondered putting this book out into the world inviting people on behalf of Michael the Archangel to use his Divine sword, I didn't need to go through the manuscript and highlight in color all the new information, which there is plenty of. This book basically wrote itself, like never before, as I received validation upon validation *as the book unfolded* and in perfect timing. I learned not only the extreme significance of the sword, but why we are at this very juncture now that we are being asked to use it. We can choose to use our free will and join forces with the highest of the high, as we take action for the Light. Again, the Heavens can only interfere so much. It is up to us to use our free will to become Archangel Michael's Warriors of Light.

October 18, 2017

*The greater you see and understand what is really occurring on Earth, and has been most especially in recent decades, the harder it may feel to endure. And yet I tell you, the way out of this dark grip on precious life is through truth. Truth—really exposing and understanding the torment forced on humanity—will free you from the chains of imprisonment you have endured, while the majority are mostly or completely unaware.*

*Your courage to seek the truth has never been more needed as you are at a breaking point and turning point. Breaking point as the confusion is so wide and rampant, and often by design. And turning point because you are turning the corner on massive revealing of so much darkness that has plagued your Earth. I say this not to frighten you but to ask you to bravely seek and allow the truths to be revealed both in the macrocosm and microcosm. For when you allow the truths of your personal lives to be set free, that in turn affects the greater and more global truths to be set free as well.*

*When you learn the truth about a dangerous product, say, you are empowered with information that convinces you to avoid that product. When you learn the truths that have been, are being, or are about to be revealed on a much more massive scale, you will clearly be making new choices which will have a dynamic and profound effect on and for the betterment for humanity, that which only truth can bring. So, seek the truth... in all ways. Bring this actual word 'truth' into your inner and outer vocabulary every day. This is part of the spiritual warrior's way.*

On October 22, 2017, Michael gave me a personal message but also meant to be shared:

*You are uncovering huge, huge information, Mary. You will be empowering people to take part in shifting this planet Earth. As you know our first book together was about creating Heaven on Earth, and the next step now is to help people to take active roles in this process. For every person who takes part, it will have a magnified effect, so please know that. For each person who hears their soul's call to join the spiritual revolution and transmute all darkness into Light, their efforts will not only be magnified, but they will have reach not just in the present and thus future, but in the past, as well. The Earth will be moving toward a new experience as it leaves shackles upon shackles behind and absorbs such immense Light that it will be able to birth the new, a new Earth, an Earth beyond your imaginings.*

October 23, 2017
*We hear the cries of many of you. "Enough... Enough!" you say. "How much more do you think we can take?" "Help us, Heavens! I cannot take anymore!" And I tell you we hear each of you, and we will not "sugar coat" any of this. You are enduring such difficult, often harrowing times especially depending on what parts of the world you are from or what your personal challenges are. We wish we*

*could take away your worries, your pain, your extreme challenges during these times. You are on a planet of free will and that makes it impossible for us to interfere where permission is not granted. We do step in, we absolutely do, to ensure things do not go too far or cause irreparable damage. Know that irreparable to the Earth's occupants is different than irreparable is as the Heavens' hierarchy sees it. As there are technologies that humanity is not aware of, that can and are being used and often.*

*The key here is free will. The key is to not only remember to ask for help, but to empower yourself with your free will and take the action that must be taken now. You, humans, please remember as you have heard many times. You are true co-creators of this new world. And you are now needed to 'step up to the plate' like never before. Check in within your heart now. Do you feel this call? Do you know that this was all part of the plan of co-creation but you are entering more intense times now and need to be proactive like never before? I do not want this to at all sound like doom and gloom for that cannot be further from the truth. You are bringing forth Heaven onto Earth. YOU are the change-makers and YOU will help change this planet forevermore. On a planet with lower energetic vibrations, the efforts are expected to be more intense than on one that holds higher energetic vibrations.*

*Oh, if you could see the scores of souls working with you from this vantage point. You are far from alone, everything is seen and monitored, and I will remind you again, the plan is in place and cannot be altered. It is merely when, not if, your planet will shift into a higher frequency and live on in ways beyond what you can even imagine. So please hold onto relentless faith as I've asked of you many times. In your sleep, we remind you. Sometimes you have awful dreams and nightmares as you clear your pasts and ancient pasts. Other times you wake extremely refreshed, positive, and renewed as we help you emotionally detach and break free from the constant stress of everyday life. We are helping you in your dream state quite often, as well as your waking state. You may or may not remember what occurred, but you may just know or feel that something positive happened. This is the way of these times. You are also being constantly rejuvenated either through the self, through others around you as we often send you reminders through messengers, and directly through your connections with the Heavens. The spirit, the spirit itself is so strong and something to be tapped into via your hearts. I cannot ever talk enough about this as it is the key to your new way of living and being. It is the disconnect between humans and their hearts that bring a negative and persistently challenging reality for you. Shift that and you will shift your outlook as you tap into your greatest power—your heart.*

October 25, 2017

*Dear Spiritual Warriors. I am calling you forth to exercise what you ultimately came here at this momentous time on Earth to do. To be Warriors of Light! The Earth and its occupants are at a point where Light must be spread and darkness yield to its power and hold, for the mayhem must stop! If by now you don't know what is really going on, the raping and pillaging of life, in nearly every area and aspect of life, you need to know now. If you agree to be a Warrior of Light you also need to know what is really occurring behind the scenes. We see all and we tell you that despite various deceptive teachings, action is needed on this free will planet. You don't need to know every detail, and it is preferred that you do not get caught up in it as it can lower your vibration, but rather have a basic understanding so you know where to spread the Light, where to extend the sword. And all of this done from a higher perspective is key.*

*As you extend your sword, you do so with the intention of firmly addressing the darkness itself and transmuting that energy that can no longer remain. Your intention and co-partnering with me is your most significant role now. I ask you to practice using the sword every day. Start small and work on yourself. Once you see the power we have together, you will be more than inspired to address the big issues on your planet.*

*The prayers you are already sending to your planet do help, any intention from the heart helps. But the sword, using the sword with me, will have an effect that you have not seen before. For you will be in warrior mode, albeit a peaceful warrior, but do not confuse peaceful with lack of strength. When I yield the sword, it creates various change depending on each situation. It is energetic, but is more real than anything you see on Earth with the physical eyes.*

*If you want peace for your planet, raise your sword to the dark creating chaos everywhere, including war. If you want health for your family and friends, for all living things, raise your sword to the dark that has created a myriad of health issues through food and many other means. If you want clear and normal skies again, raise your sword to the dark that is poisoning them. If you want freedom, finally, on this planet, then raise your sword to the darkness that has enslaved you. It is time to stand up and create the necessary change now!*

*When you free yourself in the Now, you change the past and ancient past of humans enslaved, for example. Anything you raise the sword to, you will shift its history, as well. That history will become obsolete in the new Earth.*

Following this message, Michael asked me to search the word "obsolete" in the word documents of my two other channeled books with him. I came across this channeled message from Indira Gandhi in *The New Sun*[4]:

*This channel is surprised that I am coming through, for she doesn't really know anything about me as a former leader in India, and she at first thought I was Mahatma Gandhi. But it is me, Indira Gandhi, former prime minister of India, and I have an important message. Forgive your leaders, your past political leaders, all those who have had tremendous responsibilities and power and in many ways led this world further from love, rather than toward it. As you read these words, specific names will come to mind, perhaps mine among them. It may even bring up anger and your body may tense, and that is not my intention, although it may be a necessary step in the process of letting go of the past, in this way, as well. Forgive our mistakes, often*

---

[4] Soliel, Mary. *The New Sun.* Boulder: Twelve Twelve Publishing, LLC, 2013.

*horrific mistakes. Forgive our straying from God's will and rather enforcing our own will, or the will of those with lower vibrations that have wreaked havoc on countless lives as well as the Earth herself. Both individual and collective energies created karma that plague not only people, but regions, countries, and all that is. As you move toward peace on this planet, this karma will be released. You can help this process through your forgiveness and higher under-standing.*

I appreciate how these understandings come full circle. Because she then ended the message with just what Michael is talking about now: *One day, these will be distant memories and a very old and obsolete history, because you will be in a very new existence. So, let go and let God. Be well and free.*

October 26, 2017

*A most vital part of raising the sword and using my sword with me, is that you own your power. You must raise your frequency to own the whole of your powerful self. You may need to use your imagination or you can naturally own your own recognized power. Either way, at least in time you will eventually get to this point, with your sword work, to acknowledge and work with your magnificence which knows no limitations. Yes, it's time to move past any limit-ations that have limited your movement, abilities, practices, and ways of being on your Earth. When you call me forth to work with the sword, see us at the same level; again, use your imagination if needed.*

*When you really own your power, it may frighten some away who will feel it on some level. Do not let this stop your work, for relationships are going through a vulnerable and often more challenging period right now, no matter what you do, no matter what power you hold. It does not serve you or the world to hide or lessen your power. Please own who you really are. As you grow closer to your souls and led by who you really are, you change this world. It simply cannot be done without you. Oh, the intricacies of all that is coming together to shift this Earth, the higher vibrational children being born into the world, the increasing energies that reveal greater glimpses of Heaven as the veils thin, the relentless devotion of Lightworkers working so hard to spread awareness and Light. Nothing will stop this necessary shift of your planet, but, again, everyone has their part to play and now.*

October 27, 2017

*Co-creators! You will have unlimited abilities at your disposal when you choose to take the sword. When I say abilities, I'm not necessarily talking about specific talents or gifts, I'm talking specifically about your abilities to make change occur in a multitude of ways. When you raise the sword "to the sky," you will on some level be "in the sky" with my sword and with me. When you raise your sword to specific places on your planet where darkness has resided, a part of you will be there right next to me. When you raise your sword in protection of the abandoned and rejected, a part of you will be existing among them for that moment, with me by your side.*

*Can you use your imagination to see, literally feel your presence wherever you raise your sword? When this channel does healing work, say over a region of the world experiencing tragedy or potential tragedy, she sees her body in flight, enlarged many times its size, and the Light from the New Sun and the Heavens flows through her body and onto the targeted territory to receive the Light. You can do the same. You must believe in the power you have, beyond anything you ever have before. Let go of all limitations in order to do this work. And your imagination may be the vehicle of choice to "take you there." Do not question the limitlessness of your soul which will be in the captain's seat.*

This way of channeling the Light just naturally surfaced during my travels when I did extensive healing work, where I felt energy was needed. I would suddenly just send my beingness into the sky, enlarge myself to an immense size in my imagination to span the whole area that is intended to receive, and become the receptacle for Light from the New Sun to be sent right through me. Know that this is the Divine Light energy we will work with for our sword work, to be described in Chapter Six. In those moments, I let go of my insecurities, beliefs, and 3D vision of myself. I elevate myself beyond the known, and this is what Michael is asking all of us to do now, each in our own creative ways.

October 29, 2017

*Dear Spiritual Warriors, if you have read this far, would it mean that you are serious about taking on this role? Somehow you were led to this book, either through connection to the channel, connection to others recommending it, or, ultimately, through synchronicity. You were drawing the empowered information to you. And empowered it is, for you will be in the most powerful position you have ever been in to create positive change in this world. How can this not be so? My sword is being extended to you, and you know in the depth of your being you have not only been waiting for this, but you have been prepared for this. This channel keeps saying, "the house of cards is falling," and this is true. The sword will expedite this process, but also, and this is a most important part of the process, the energy of the dark will be transmuted via the sword. Yet, I will remind you again and again, this work must be done with a level of emotional detachment. If you raise the sword with anger and hatred, that will not work. Can you imagine that is how I use the sword? I use it for a shift to righteousness, to cover in Divine Light. If you mix negative energy in there, the effect would not be powerful; in fact, it will not serve the situation and thus will not be allowed. This will be challenging when you raise the sword certainly in personal situations, so be sure to have me right with you, to help you stay out of negative emotions. You must stand way above the situation for real change to take place. The world is quickly waking up to the fact that wars and aggression do not work. They keep the world mired in the lowest of vibrations. And all in the name of "patriotism." That word will have new meaning when countries shift their energy to true service to a unified world. It is the Divine Feminine energies that will save your world, not the extreme masculine energies that have tried to destroy it. Again, male and female energies are present in all males and females! And you are rebalancing these energies. But the extreme and destructive male energies that have gotten out of control over eons of time, the depth of this extreme is to a degree not readily understood. Be aware but do not focus on this. Just know that you are making real change happen. This will all be on an invisible level, and your efforts may not be seen or appreciated on an earthly level, most likely, but they will be from Heaven's perspective! You are among the greatest heroes of this time for standing up for the Light and raising the sword for Light, truth, and protection. You are taking on the role of angel, can you see this now? You do your work in a balanced and detached way. You do so without needing credit or something in return. You do all of this because of unconditional love and forgiveness that resides in your heart. This work will grow your soul like nothing before because you are working on the level of an angel. Does this sound too grandiose to you? If not, I congratulate you for you are ready to really step into the magnificence that you are. This is what happens when you grow closer to your souls. You become who you really are which is Divine magnificence.*

I could feel Michael's words above so deeply. It came out so effortlessly and with even further resolve to do this very work. His words, his signs upon signs, his messages through other people are all valuable to no end. He knew I would need this, all of this, to have the courage to write this unique book declaring his new clarion call. And by the same token, it is all meant to be shared with you, the whole story, so that you have the courage to do this work as well. I truly have kept every necessary part of this story here in these pages; nothing vital to your knowing is left out.

A few hours after channeling this message, I happened upon the most perfect and validating meme on Facebook. My friend Stephenie had posted this image. It was extremely rare that I saw an image of a woman with a sword before this mission unfolded, and suddenly images of swords, even held by women, are everywhere. And here Michael just said: *It is the Divine Feminine energies that will save your world, not the extreme masculine energies that have tried to destroy it.*

The Divine Feminine
Has Been
Reawakened
On the Planet.

In Other Words,

"Mama's Home."

Source of Facebook post unknown

I commented under the photo asking where my friend got this amazing image as there was no website or logo on it. She said "sorry, no idea. I just had it in saved photos." Yes, it stayed in her saved photos for the most perfect timing to be shared!

And yes, with "Mama home," we are and will be seeing "the house of cards" really fall. We knew this would be coming so let's raise the sword again and again for the hidden truths to be revealed like never before. The dark energies are being transmuted, or at least cast out, with his sword of Light.

Just before this posting, Rhonda tagged me in a post on Facebook with pictures of her and her dog at Lake Louise for a return trip after our time together. She wrote: "AAM is all around us!!" Yet more and more validation. Michael is sending winks to and through many.

On this very day a year prior, I had a personal channeled message from Archangel Michael, in telepathic conversational style as that is how we usually communicate. When I channel him, I always type as I'm receiving, conversing with him.

Mary: Michael, I am having a hard time watching what is occurring on so many levels, especially the continued manipulations and deceptions, and so many people, even Lightworkers, are "buying" it! I used to "buy" it, but cannot any longer. There is no going back... I never want to go back to being unaware. And as much as I'm aware, of course there is so very much I don't know.

*Mary, you have had 22 years of, shall we call it "inside information."*

Mary: And it still took a long while for me to see, but now I want to see everything so I can help transmute and shift it, among the many doing the same.

*You and others like you who are aware of truths, what is really going on, or have desires to get to the truth and who are brave enough to get to those truths, are having a very difficult time now. But this will cease, for you are being transformed at a rate faster than you can imagine.*

Mary: I feel it, Michael, I feel it. And I feel so out of this world right now. I'm finding it difficult to get grounded.

*It is very hard to be in this world right now when you see such continuation of the same calamities, the same manipulations, the same corruption—and it's escalating... however... However, it will not stay this way. It cannot stay this way. No matter how many people are still yet unawakened, nothing is stopping the Light, nothing. It may affect the timing, but not the end result.*

Mary: This is why we are being guided to help spread the awareness, to help tip the scales sooner rather than later!

*Yes, and thank you for just trusting that. For you to really understand it, I would have to pluck you from your world to see the way that we see, what is coming, what is ahead. Just trust, trust, trust that all will be well in ways beyond your imagining, but until then, these are not easy times. We understand that and we are here for you. You know to come to us without hesitation.*

*Please take care of yourself, please put yourself first. You're finally learning this lesson as you struggle with it, with the type of heart you have. This was a tough one for you, and it is for everyone to master on your plane.*

Mary: Thank you, Michael. I love you so much.

Further, on this day I was inspired to write the following: "The truths, the Truths, the TRUTHS... it is time. The more we know of the darkness that has resided among us (and while staying out of fear and seeing from a higher perspective), that is so incredibly in our faces now in so many ways, the more we can positively affect life, the Earth, each other from a new foundation of what is real."

"As we grow our authentic selves, shedding what is not serving us in the microcosm, we eventually move into an authentic world in the macrocosm where love rules and peace is the norm. May we focus on staying the course and allowing the truths to be revealed. Bring it on."

I thought it was me, Mary, writing these words but clearly Michael was behind them. Sometimes I don't know where I stop and Michael starts. We are a partnership and it is a partnership that anyone can have with him or any of the highest of the high. You may already know just what I mean, with your own similar partnerships, certainly with a great number of you also connected to Archangel Michael. You will most definitely experience this partnership if you choose to take Michael's sword!

Michael taught me something very significant a year ago which has stuck with me. He said that the macrocosm is affected by the microcosm of our lives and vice versa. So, what you may be healing in your life is affecting the world, the Universe. That's why he always says, everything you do "good" or "bad" is helping or hindering the world. And what is going on in the world affects us on personal levels. We're all affecting the collective. It's quite a fascinating perspective and a whole different way to look at life.

These mere words expressing the relationship between the macrocosm and microcosm changed so much of how I view and experience everything. Do you ever feel you are "taking one for the team?" That you are working through something in the microcosm which is not only helping yourself and others around you, but also the collective? It is probably because you are. When we get this, we really understand oneness and how we are all Divinely and intricately connected. We also own just how powerful we are.

October 30, 2017

*At this point in your understanding of the sword I am asking you to increase your connect to it via your heart. You see, it is your heart, your soul, that is driving this mission. You cannot do this work without this most vital connection. You cannot raise the sword without being in connection with the compassion and love that reside in your heart. You cannot even use the sword without this connection, for it will hold no power. So, when you raise the sword, know that your heart is in line with this process, for it has to be this way.*

*Your heart is leading the way. It will guide you to the right areas to focus on at the right times. I have taught many times that you simply must connect with your heart, literally communicate with it, as your greatest wisdom comes from there. Not outside of you, it is all within you. So feel that power, trust it. For it will reveal all you need to stay centered and secure in this mission.*

*When you connect with your heart, you are also connecting with us there. We meet you there, in the pureness of you. So, this is your respite from fears, worries, concerns, confusion, or anything else that could possibly arise in this work. Put your hand on your heart, tune in, and meet us there. We are always there for you, something you don't experience to this degree on the Earth plane. As you work with us in this way, you learn to trust this connection and count on us as we will never lead you astray. Always think of us as your team members, for we are always working together.*

*Do not feel separate as you raise the sword, feel the unity with me. And then feel the unity of others who join you in this mission. It will erase so many potential discomforts when you simply and consciously work with me. As you practice this work, you will grow your inner strength and find a power within that will grow. This is empowering work, your warrior work, and you will no longer feel helpless in a world that is in chaos. You will bring Light to the chaos. You will help shift whatever you place your Light-filled intention on. If you do not believe my words, then use your imagination until you see shifts in your own life, and in the world outside of you. Find the proof yourself.*

*Make no mistake, you have been doing so much work over many years, and it is the Lightworkers who have created many huge shifts in every aspect of life on Earth. But now, it is time to become very active as a spiritual warrior. It is taking your efforts to a much greater level and intensity by working with me and my sword. It is time and it is why you have been led to this book. The darkness has simply gotten out of control, gone way too far, and every soul who signed up to help create Heaven on Earth is needed like never before to shift these dark energies once and for all.*

November 2, 2017

*This channel is gaining more and more confidence in her mission. She is constantly surprised by how this mission, for the most part, has unfolded effortlessly by simply being aware, following her guidance, and trusting her intuition. And let me tell you, the same will happen for you, those of you who join her on this mission. You will feel wonderfully blessed with revelations, miracles, synchronicities, and deep inner resolve to do this work, as well.*

*So yes, be strong and confident. If you slip into fear, simply call on me. Remember, you will never do this work alone. You cannot use the sword by yourself, even though you stand there in the physical holding the sword perhaps just with self. I am always there. I AM Archangel Michael... consciously align yourself with me, dear soul. For I am here for you and you are here for me. And together, we will make a difference in the world. Together, we will help and heal your world, and create the new template for your new Earth. As I have said before, you cannot even imagine the brilliant life ahead of you, all of you.*

*When you take my sword, raise my sword for Light, truth, and protection. With that alone, even before stated intentions, you have amassed great power and are greatly pleasing us in the Heavens. When you grow your awareness, and accept the darkness of your realities, you are greatly respected for your resolve and courage. Raise the sword feeling our respect. Elevate yourselves, not from the ego but from the heart, fully knowing and stepping into who you really are. Feel the power that is you, as you align yourself with this Archangel.*

*This channel gets frustrated when people ask her to say "hello" to Michael for them. For she knows that I hear them as well as I hear her. I am here for everyone, as she has proclaimed for years. She wants people to talk to me directly as that is what I wish and have stated time and time again. Talk to me! Share your joy, your pain, your questions, your concerns. Grow our bond and it will help you connect with the sword work. Grow your sword work and it will help you connect with me, in general.*

My cell phone's light flickered on for no reason as I ended this channel which made me tap it, and then saw that it was 11:11! As many of us know, our angels wink at us in these ways. This was for you.

November 4, 2017

*Dear ones, for you are so dear to us. Your courage and resolve to help this world rather than just throwing up your arms is unprecedented. You are being faced with so much, things you are not even aware of on a conscious level, but it is still there. And yet, you persevere. Why? Because you know that you are here just for this, to be the spiritual warriors needed to shift the direction your Earth has been headed for eons of time. Out of control power, corruption, and, yes, evil forces have taken over the planet, and you are now fighting back in larger numbers every day—with the force of love, the force of Light. These two words, love and Light, are often thrown around in what you may deem as 'syrupy' expressions, but the truth is these words hold more power than any other.*

*People take love and distort it, as I have said before. But when love is in its authentic form, everything pales in its presence. This is why you are called to be spiritual Warriors of Light, with love as your power source. You have sifted through so much of your "baggage" and healed so much so that you, as a living soul on Earth, could be love in a most authentic way. To not just throw that word around but to really feel and know love like you never have.*

*When you feel unconditional love for someone, most especially someone who has hurt you deeply, as then and only then in the midst of such pain can you see what love looks like without distortion, without the irrelevant games or misunderstandings. For that love is so pure, it is a gift to experience. That is the love we feel for you, no matter what. And that is love that you all must learn to feel for yourselves. Pure love because that is what you really are.*

Ironically (or not really), after Michael's message, I realized that on this very day six years ago, I was interviewed on The Sam Lesante Show (which can be seen on my YouTube channel: MarySoliel). I felt to listen to the recording of it. When Sam asked me to provide some examples of synchronicity, I described when I was deeply hurt by a friend and shortly after was awed by a stunning synchronicity that made me realize I needed to forgive immediately, even before I had the chance to process what occurred.

A dog ran in front of my car at the same moment I heard song lyrics about forgiveness (the dog was fine). I explained to Sam that this sign taught me not only did I need to forgive this person right away, but I needed to *reside in this state of unconditional love and forgiveness*. To create a more peaceful world, we need to release the anger, hatred, all these things that are keeping our hearts chained up, and rather fully open up our hearts. Our most vital lesson is unconditional love and forgiveness, for ourselves and others. It's the way to our new Earth. There's nothing more important, and this is the lifetime to really get this—to reside in this place.

November 5, 2017

*You are seeing and will be seeing the world in a whole new way. As the darkness is revealed, you will grieve for all the damage, the unknown effects, the repetitive harm—in some cases, for centuries. It will literally uproot your life and propel you into a new awareness with resolve to make things right in your world. There will be a gathering of souls to unearth it all, to turn things upside down, for only then can you build this promised Heaven on Earth. The darkness can no longer reside on this planet so even though your hearts will ache for those affected, which is really and truly every single one of you, the focus must be on the reveal and the rebuild. This will be the most creative time on Earth. The creative aspects of you will be shining forth as you co-create your new Earth.*

*You will feel more connected to others than you ever have. You won't feel people are strangers; you will honor and respect them with immediacy, always seeing the very best in people. You accept peoples' beliefs and ways, even when they do not mesh with yours. You allow people to be who they are. You don't have to socialize and open up to an active relationship with everyone by all means. As I've said many times, you must watch your energy and be choosy in who you "surround yourself" with so that you stay strong. But this is all about unity, unifying with others for a common theme, a common goal, to protect the Earth and all life that resides on it. The energy of division doesn't mesh with where you are headed.*

*So I ask you to be easier on others and do not berate or hate others, for the energy of hate does not mesh with where you are headed. That includes the dark of the dark. When you hate, it breeds more of the energy of hate. Just focus on the reveal and standing up for life, for the Earth. The horrors are innumerable and unconscionable. And yet, the Earth will no longer be able to support these atrocities nor the people who create them. Do you see why there is no point in wasting energy on emotion, but rather put your energies on the end of the darkness on your planet?*

*I, Archangel Michael, do not hate those that I battle. They must be stopped but if I expelled the energy of hate, that is war-like, the type of war that occurs on Earth. I am only about love. And love can, does, and will transform the world. My sword is about Love, ultimately, and even when I wield it, it is with the force of Love. Anything else would have no lasting consequence. My sword lights the way to transmutation and transformation of these dark energies. Thus, the requirement for detachment is vitally important. Again, when you raise the sword it is vital to stay in the highest space of Light and love and I will be there to help you do this.*

*Battles of Light vs. dark are a necessary part of life on Earth to create your new Earth. It is also a necessary act to protect life from Heaven's perspective, to lessen the effects of such extreme darkness on your free will planet. But war carries no Light. Wars on Earth have been created in the name of darkness in reality, but often falsely advertised in the name of God or Light or some other made up connection. There is nothing about physical war that is connected to Creator. Nothing. Love would never choose war. It will choose spiritual battle when necessary, and we are in these times now.*

November 6, 2017

*My spiritual warriors, your willingness to join me in changing this world in a quiet and yet absolutely powerful way is essential to your future. This was always part of the plan, to offer the sword to those ready for this most vital mission. I ask you to face your fears which will make you stronger. Sometimes facing difficulty is necessary in order to grow your power. This channel knows this all too well. For she faced the darkness and came out on the other side. Had she not experienced what she had, she simply could not write this book. Think of the most powerful messages you've ever heard, they are often about beings facing adversity and allowing it to change them for the better. So, no matter what you have gone through, it is perfectly setting you up to be able to take the sword and raise it in the name of Light.*

*Do you think many would be willing to pick up my sword had they not been subjected to all the ails of the Earth? Had they not seen too many people suffer and lose their lives due to dark influences? Had they not witnessed such assault on the environment? And on and on. You are at the point where you say "Enough!" You know you must take an active role and the sword is now being offered to you. Know that as you do this work in silence, its effects will be loud and far reaching. This is where your faith will come in.*

*You will see changes in your personal life when you raise the sword, and this will give you the confidence to raise it for worldly issues. You will exercise that muscle of faith, knowing you are making a grand difference. This work will transform you, for you are stepping into your power and with what I refer to as relentless faith. It is the only way. You must hold that faith no matter what future challenges will arise. For there will be future challenges, as it will take time to shift the deep-rooted darkness.*

*Open your eyes, though, to what is in front of you. The promise of your new Earth. And you are seeing signs of it everywhere as the veil thins more and more. Do not let the dark close your eyes to the miracles of your daily existence. That is what they want. They want to break your spirit. They want you to hate and lose hope. They want you to cower to their power. So you must make their attempts futile. As soon as you fear, they take hold. But you can choose again and again until you face any fears and dissolve them. Again, always keep me by you, along with my sword, and allow me to help you stay strong. You are aligned with me and I am aligned with you. Let us be in this space of peace and strength together.*

On this same day, I read a passage from a spiritual leader that there is a clarion call and it is urgent. Then, my friend Donna sent me the link to a song written for the Black Hills Unity Concert www.TheUnityConcert.com, which raised my eyebrows at the following lyrics: "The battle has only just begun and Creator is sending His very best warriors." It says that the only weapons in this battle are weapons of truth, faith, and compassion. How perfect a confirmation is this? I am just gobsmacked by more and more validating winks, for you and me!

November 7, 2017

*Come and gather around this campfire, imagine it in your mind. You, those of you carrying the sword, are mighty and charged to get out there and use your free will and power to make a difference. But let's just "group" together for now. Just be in touch with all who are also committed to this very work. Embrace each other, feel the teamwork, the unity, the coming together to save your planet. Let this fuel you, let it charge you up! For there is always strength in numbers, so when you go out and do this work, remember, there are others working for the same cause. It is important to really feel this.*

*One day you will know each other by name. You will meet on the "other side" and will recognize each other as the Lightbearers who completed their mission of spreading the Light, demanding the truth, and protecting the Earth and its inhabitants. But for now, just remember that you are not alone in this. For there will be many joining this Light brigade. This was all planned and you are needed now, more than ever.*

*This is not easy work and at times you may feel you have the world on your shoulders. And that's why I want you to recognize that you are not alone, whatsoever. The weight of responsibility is outshined by the power of the sword. You come to realize its magical and robust qualities. It will never let you down. It will only lift you up. But your faith is required at all times.*

It is exactly one month to the day that I returned from Canada to begin working on this book, in earnest. I nearly have a rough draft of this manuscript thanks to Michael's magical unfolding— constantly inspired and fueled by his guidance, messages, and synchronicity itself. Everything is coming together with much ease—aside from the more difficult things I must write about.

November 11, 2017

*Dear ones, dear courageous beings agreeing to set your sights and energies on shifting your world, for it needs every one of you. Why have I asked you to take this new role now? Because it is time. The time is perfectly ripe for your efforts to have grand effects. Had you taken on this role too early, it would have backfired. But the darkness is weakening, they are losing their stronghold. Oh yes, they are still causing much mayhem nearly everywhere you look, but their foundations are cracking. This is not news to this channel for we have referenced cracking foundations to her before, beneath those places that were and are needing to fall apart. Well, let the cracking continue. Had you done this work before the cracking was this evident, it would not have bowed well, but let's just say that the collective darkness is experiencing pockets of cracks and as the cracks build and grow, and their vibrations lower even more as the Earth's vibration increases, they will experience increasing chaos. Do you see that they forced chaos on you, the Earth, all living beings? And now the pendulum swings as it must, and chaos will be theirs as the dark leaves. There is a lot that must be done. And as you see the unveiling and falling of that which does not serve your planet, it will rejuvenate and inspire you to continue on with this process, stepping into your power and your free will to shift this Earth.*

*Do not fear! You are always protected. In the past, you would pray or do energy work to shift the dark's attempts and practices. This is just a different way of addressing what can no longer continue on Earth. And with the power of you and me together. Do you see how this is the time now? Do you feel it? While this channel has stayed away from the sword and always avoided words like battle, there is no way to avoid it anymore and she now sees it very differently. Perhaps you feel the same way. The difference is, in this battle you are protected, just as you are protected when you say a prayer, for there really is no difference. But you are taking on a most active role for the Light and before God. It is time.*

November 13, 2017

Throughout my life, I have held little interest in history, mythology, and even folklore. To be honest, I've mostly avoided learning things of the past that most people know about. I am here for the present and the future, and while I may draw on history, because we hopefully learn from our mistakes, or we need to know the past to understand the present, I otherwise know so little.

It was my daughter who shared with me the legend of the Sword in the Stone, a couple of months after I was offered Michael's sword. I was indeed familiar with the name of the tale and the figures in it, but never knew the simple and yet powerful story. As the legend goes, Merlin said that only the one able to pull the magical sword from the stone—which he placed in an anvil—would be fit to rule England, rescuing the country from its chaos. When Merlin brought Arthur before the sword, and after Arthur was able to easily pick up the sword, he became crowned the King of England.

You are hopefully making the association here. If you who are of the Light, of true and honorable intentions utilizing Light and love as we co-create our new Earth, you too will be able to pick up the sword—Michael's sword!

It was fitting that my daughter sent me this link www.heroofcamelot.com/legend/sword-in-the-stone which had the most revealing reference about Merlin: "Having seen to it that baby Arthur was safe, he erected a large stone, on top of which sat an anvil, in a churchyard in Westminster, a region of London." Dear readers, as I write this, I am temporarily living in Westminster! When I was called to pick up Michael's sword, I was truly living in Westminster, Colorado. I'm preparing to move now, but the fact is I was here in a synchronous place at the perfect time.

After my reading with Jeannie today, I was clearly guided to take a walk by Standley Lake. I hadn't visited for weeks—yet was there on the perfect day. I pondered the synchronicity with Westminster, while walking, making a mental note to myself to include this in the book. And what do I come across?

"Congratulations! Westminster." Can you feel the auspiciousness of this very random find of a green glass egg with this note (from the lake's park), and the timing of it? This kind of magic and much more will be yours when you raise the sword! Archangel Michael is showing us the way and will bless you, too, with blissful signs to give you strength and resolve.

With so much coming forth about Merlin and King Arthur, I did some research and came across a documentary on YouTube: "The Truth Behind King Arthur." The video begins with a picture of a sword planted in stone. At one point, an anthropologist talks about the "Lady of the Lake" legend in the King Arthur story.

The Lady of the Lake offers the sword Excalibur to Arthur. It's a sword that is held in a magical hand in the middle of the water, as pictured. I instantly made the connection to the inverted cloud (page 42) I saw at Okanagan Lake, depicting what I eventually realized was a floating hand holding a sword handle!

Note: A few weeks later, while I was watching a video on YouTube.com, I *heard* to watch a video that was listed as "Up next" on my home page. It was "King Arthur," a TLC documentary narrated by Richard Harris, the actor who played King Arthur in the Hollywood musical *Camelot*.

Richard distinguished the two famous sword stories in this way: "But the sword in the stone is only one of two great swords in the story. One day, when he was fully grown into a man, Arthur needed a new sword. Merlin told him where he could find a magical blade fit for a king. In a secret lake lived an underwater enchantress, the Lady of the Lake. She controlled the most powerful sword of all, Excalibur. Now there's a fantasy image. But there may be an element of truth in it. Archeologists in Britain have found countless ancient sword blades. Guess where? At the bottom of lakes and rivers."

Archeologist Francis Pryor added: "I think actually placing swords in water is part of a right of passage." I immediately recalled when Rhonda brought me the wooden sword, gifted by Michael, after she dipped it in Moraine Lake along with the crystal. I can still see her balancing the twin crystal (two terminations, or points, on one end— perhaps symbolic of Arthur's two swords) on the sword after having bathed both in the water, and walking it over to me. Was Rhonda ceremonially performing a rite of passage without realizing it? At the time, it really struck me to the point I felt to add this in the book when I returned from Canada, weeks before knowing about the legend.

With the Westminster synchronicity, along with the inverted cloud of the sword in the hand literally while at a lake in Kelowna, and now the

Lady of the Lake synchronicity, everything feels so magically symbolic and mystical. It's as if Rhonda was representing the Lady of the Lake, presenting me with the sword from the water. And the funny thing is she kept saying that she wanted to be *in* the water. I find myself wanting to perform this ceremony for all you spiritual Warriors of Light accepting Michael's sword—I now believe I will, at least in spirit!

Two days after watching this documentary, I was on a Skype call with Mia, and she randomly asked if I knew of the "Lady of the Lake." Not only was I shocked that she brought her up, but she said she had never heard of her and the legend until one or two months ago. I told her that I, too, hadn't heard of her until one or two months ago!

Michael said through Jeannie, before my trip to Canada, that things would open up as if by magic upon my return, and they sure have, especially with mystical validations such as those described.

November 20, 2017

This evening proved most significant. For the first time, I felt the energy running through my arm. Here I had completed the rough draft of this book, as much as I could write at this point as I work more with the sword, train with it. The difference tonight is that I succeeded with techniques to remain neutral when using the sword, to take the emotion out of it. The surprise was that the energy came through my left arm and I am right-handed.

I felt a pulsing on for a few seconds and then off for a few seconds, on and off—running down my forearm, mostly felt in my wrist to upper hand. I am filled with excitement as I knew it was only a matter of time before I would feel it. I asked Archangel Michael to address what just occurred.

*Mary, for you have just experienced the first taste of transference of power and it will not stop now. So, wherever you intend Light, truth, and protection, you are always sending this energy!*

Mary: I feel you giving me a huge download of information now, all at once. For instance, you are making me understand that just like I hear what I call the "God sound" in my head (a high-pitched whistle)—at all times, truly without pause now, which helps me connect to you—I will also be able to connect to this energy all the time, as well. Both are sacred gifts that connect me to you.

*You are ready now. You are unstoppable, as will be the many spiritual warriors who join you, Lightbearers from around the globe. For it is important to have many placed in the physical, from all "corners" of the Earth.*

*You are calibrating to this shift so just give it time. Work with this, understand it, embrace it into your being. Nothing will ever be the same from this point on as you now carry this energy from your Archangel and for always. You have been protected, you are protected, and so will all who join you in this mission.*

Mary: My whole body is tingling, especially in my head and both feet now.

*You know that your life will be full of great change from this point. You welcome change, you always have... you are a rare one, and one of the reasons why you were chosen for this.*

Mary: It's as if I cannot even think of what's wrong in my life in this moment, I do not care, I feel way above my 3D life, and I like this feeling very much. I know that one day we will all be feeling this constantly.

Mary: It has been about an hour now and I still feel high on this energy. I feel so lifted, feeling the energy even more so. I feel stronger than ever and impenetrable by anything but this wonderful energy. I cannot hold a negative thought now, even if I tried.

The next day:

Mary: Today was a whirlwind. The very thing I raised the sword for—as per your guidance after I felt the energy coming through last night—it surely got illuminated! I know this happened for many reasons, not the least of which was to prove how powerful this is. There was a chain of events that put a spotlight on a growing issue.

*As you know, everything happens for a reason and because of your faith in this work, you made a big shift occur. You saw and experienced it in such a way, you cannot doubt the power of the sword.*

Mary: When fellow spiritual warriors see how the sword works in their personal lives, it will grow their faith and excitement in this. It will build our faith for the vital work we do for the collective and the Earth.

*Yes, because you cannot see what we see, and so your faith is very key. But many of you will feel what you accomplish and create. And we will communicate and show you signs verifying this. For instance, you will be led to information that shows that something has shifted or you will simply hear or feel our cries of joy and gratitude.*

December 4, 2017

Today, I had one more session with Jeannie prior to publication. I told her about feeling the energy surprisingly as an electrical pulse and in my left arm, and also about the feelings of bliss that accompanied it.

Michael came through Jeannie right away saying: *To truly activate the sword, it needs the heart energy, the soul. Heart and soul. So, you focused on it without being conscious. That heart energy, you were feeling it. Much like the beating of the heart in the physical body. This is a new technique now. So now when you use the sword, call in the heart energy.*

*I'm not asking you to focus on a particular being or particular situation. The heart is Light, it is Light energy. So, you can and should remain in that neutral place, always, but it's calling in the love or just opening to the pure and simple love, without being conscious of anyone in particular, or any particular situation.*

*You are opening yourself to just the love, and understand this. Love is power. Love is pure Light. It is simply pure Light. Nothing is more pure than love. So, the sword and the heart work together.*

Mary: So, this should be a step in the book for everyone, that they should call on their heart energy.

*You are correct. But also make it very apparent that they are not focusing on anything, just the light and love of the heart.*

Mary: So we should call this forth every time we use the sword?

*It is a practiced skill for those who choose to take up the sword, those who are called. Getting in that neutral place is a skill. So yes, in the beginning it needs to be conscious. But after repetition, it becomes just natural.*

How beautiful is this? The gift of the sword and all it will bring forth in both our inner and outer lives feels utterly monumental. And this blissful state of love that we achieve just prior to raising the sword is so rich and beautiful—you really feel the power that love is! I ponder how just accessing this state alone on a daily basis, even before using the sword, will positively affect each of us. It wasn't long before I realized that this bliss I felt just before raising the sword was the same bliss I felt many times before, when I spontaneously went into an ecstatic state and felt immense love within.

This feeling is similar to the ecstasy felt when experiencing an orgasm, but it is felt *throughout* the body instead of originating in the sexual organs. It is sacred ecstasy. Michael taught us in *Michael's Clarion Call* that this energy is similar to the energy that those in Heaven feel. Michael describes in this book how to actually draw forth this ecstasy through concentrated breath, which you can use when connecting to the heart in your sword work.

*Right now, focus on your breath. As you breathe in slowly and fully, imagine breathing in ecstasy, whatever that means to you. If you are not sure what it would feel like, just use your imagination of what ecstasy would feel like. Yes, and then breathe out, but getting ready to breathe in more ecstasy. As you begin to feel ecstatic feelings through your being, expect more as you breathe in again and again, and let the feelings build. Imagine you are breathing in a taste of Heaven. Know that you are allowing God's love to fill you and let the feelings flood you completely—every cell of your body and every aspect of your being. Let it take over and just keep allowing the feelings of ecstasy to run through you.*

*Now, the next time you have feelings of upset or frustration, or when you are fighting change in your life, breathe in the taste of Heaven. As you do, remember what all of your present difficulties are moving you toward; they are moving you toward the ecstasy. When you breathe in and think ecstasy on each breath, build deeper and deeper into these feelings. Let them wash over your temporary difficulties; wash them right out of your mind and just be with ecstasy.*

I just had not felt this bliss in conjunction with the sword until now, but it is all coming full circle. All of this made me think of another message in this same book from Michael which beautifully builds on this:

*There is a window that most of you humans have kept shut lifetime after lifetime. It is the window to your soul. You have been disconnected from who you really are through your earthly incarnations. But, finally, at last, you will seek to open the window to reach your soul, find communion with your soul, and meld you with you. What happens when this opportunity is finally met? You live in a state of unconditional love for yourself and all around you. That is how we create peace on Earth. As you all get in touch with your souls and live as who you really are—the eternal part of you, the part of you who residues in Heaven—peace reigns. There is no way it cannot be. Just as peace reigns in Heaven, you will create Heaven on Earth when you become you.*

While in the editing stages [of *Michael's Clarion Call*], I just re-read the above paragraph and felt something surging within me. I went into a fully ecstatic state, which came on unexpectedly. I surrendered to the experience of pure bliss traveling throughout my body. As the feelings subsided, I imagined what it will be like when we feel this internal bliss all the time, when we are in full connection with our souls. As I did so, the feelings of ecstasy fully returned.

*You may ask, "How do you connect with your soul?" I tell you that it is through feelings of love. As you raise your vibrations while living in a state of love, you naturally get to know you—the real you. Because when you take the ego, the fears, and the negative emotions away, you uncover the pearl that is you. And it is a most glorious reunion; it is a blissful state. So, intend to think, say, feel, and do all things from a state of love.*

Back to the rest of my reading with Jeannie...

Mary: As you know, I include quite a bit in the book about the dark interfering with me and others I know, as I feel awareness is crucial and I wish to help prevent readers from experiencing the same.

*It is and it is necessary. Because it helps the human mind to understand and to be aware, and how the sword can be used. So, it is necessary and thank you.*

I shared with Jeannie the excitement of feeling the electrical pulse, that I could feel the energy now.

Mary: Will I literally feel this energy in the future, every time I use the sword?

*As you work with the sword and as anyone else does as they learn, yes, you will feel it every time.*

The understanding of the gift of the sword and its power is increasing daily for me as I imagine for you, as well, as you begin this journey too. The sword will enrich our lives in limitless ways as we grow our understanding and actual experiences with drawing Michael's sword.

There will never be enough words to express my deepest gratitude to Jeannie Barnes for beautifully bringing forward all these sacred messages, which help us all.

December 6, 2017

After working on the book at a coffee shop this morning, I felt a strong urge to raise the sword. My heart, my inner compass, was telling me to do so. Suddenly, the energy was coming out the tips of the fingers in my right hand, this time. The different way the energy came through, surprised me.

I took the steps to raise the sword, as you will learn in Chapter Six. I consciously connected to my heart and went into a complete state of bliss, just as I had two weeks ago. When I raised the sword to the issue, I felt the energy so strongly and had no question of its effectiveness.

When I returned home, I wanted to document this experience in the book. As I was literally running through my mind that I would share that the sensations were coming out of my fingertips this time, and that it was more of a tingling sensation, I happened upon yet another striking synchronicity.

Once I sat with my computer, I felt to first check Facebook, and at the top of the feed was a live video. What does the woman say in the very beginning?

"Sometimes everything seems so very dire, and I really don't want you to lose heart because the solution is equally easy. It's actually a very easy solution that we all have at the tip of our fingers."

Yes, at the tip of our fingers is, literally, our easy solution! How is that for yet more synchronistic validation? She went on to say "And the solution is to live with nature as much as possible, and live with kindness every day. That's really the solution." All of this completely resonated, of course.

A few hours later, I felt to raise the sword again and as I went through the steps, I could feel the tingling in the fingertips in my right hand again, and a bit on my left as well. So far, the sensations vary each time somewhat. I sense this is temporary.

December 7, 2017

This morning, my thoughts and concerns about the devastating fires in the City of Angels took precedence. I checked a weather map of current conditions and there was no rain in the forecast; no precipitation into the Pacific either. So, I imagined rain on the radar, calling it forth. I then raised the sword while looking at the map. However, when I later closed my eyes, and imagined myself there instead, it felt even more powerful and believable. I share this as a reminder of the power of our creative imaginations. When Michael says to imagine and just *be there*, he really means it. "Imagination is more important than knowledge," said Einstein. See and feel where you are, and send the energy.

My suspicions of what was behind these fires in Los Angeles, as with other recent fires in North America, had to be tempered as I raised the sword. I had to be in that state of love without judgment or emotion. However, soon afterwards, I came across courageous truther Dane Wigington's latest weekly video update at www.geoengineeringwatch.com which substantiated that there is indeed nothing normal about these fires, as have so many other sources. *I refer to this page often for updated information on what is the most significant threat to life and our earth—geoengineering.*

If you desire to get to the truth of what is really occurring in our skies—I highly recommend Dane's updates. The updates are not easy to hear, but we must face what is really occurring. He provides the scientific backup to support his claims. Humans playing God with our climate is pure disaster and we are seeing this in innumerable ways. The atrocities of geoengineering poisoning our skies are increasingly wreaking so much havoc, including on our future ability to have basic needs of food and water. Our planet will not be able to support life if we continue on this course. We are being continually pacified, not aware of the big picture by far—and it is most serious. I believe we are receiving galactic help, but they can interfere only so much. *We simply must raise the sword to this as often as possible. Nothing matters more.*

December 8, 2017

My faith in Archangel Michael is unrelenting. As you can see from all of my sharings, I didn't even feel the energy coming through as I raised the sword until after the first rough draft of this book was completed; and yet I just kept writing. There was no question though with all that I was receiving through him, through synchronicity, through the many messages, that this was all very real and destined and I simply needed to trust the process.

Now, as soon as I feel to raise the sword, the energy, the electrical tingling or pulsing begins automatically. Sometimes it's subtle, other times quite strong. I cannot articulate to you just how this feels, and the state of love that precedes it. But I trust that you, fellow warrior, will experience it for yourself and that is actually best. I have shared all of this to inspire you but nothing is more profound than your own personal experience. May the power of raising the sword show itself in ways that will astound you, and carry you through each and every day ahead.

December 12, 2017

Today is a most special day. Two twelves represent my connection with Archangel Michael and what my publishing company is named after. On this day, I reflected on these past two months, a true whirlwind, realizing how divinely blessed this venture has been. I have never exercised trust and faith to this degree, and the resulting experiences show me it has been most well placed.

The more I raise the sword, the greater my confidence grows, and I know that the same will happen for you. When I guided my friend Mia through the steps of using the sword via a Skype call a few days ago, she immediately felt the energy coming out of her hands! This made me imagine what it will be like for each of you. I do feel I will be traveling to work with groups of people feeling the call, to help bring Michael's sword into their lives.

This brings me to another point. When I work with the sword, I imagine what it will be like when we all work with the sword on the same issue, at the same time! I feel that I will be orchestrating synchronized events to do just this. There is great power in numbers, as we know. I often think in terms of "when two or more are gathered" and feel that this will be an important part of our sword work. While I do not like the word "army," we are indeed needing to build a spiritual one!

As I write this, Michael is coming through with these words: *Do not get caught up with judgment of the common phrases of man. You are building and must build a spiritual army of Light, of love. And you are each being called to perform the sword work on your own, but then also to gather together for more profound effects. Every time you raise the sword according to the direction described in this book, and with only the highest intentions, you will be drawing forth the increasing Light filling the Earth... I do mean every time. And when you gather together, it will be even more profound as it works in an exponential way.*

*For instance, one person giving an inspiring talk to one person affects them positively. That same person speaking the same message to a hundred people will affect each of them even more profoundly. It is not just about the greater numbers, but they will benefit from the common understanding and energy between them which will heighten their individual response to the message. That will further inspire them to spread the word of this inspiring message. There is simply more energy involved which creates exponential possibilities. When you raise the sword together, you are melding your common desires for the transmutation of the dark via the Light, which will create exponential effects.*

*Do not let this lessen the solo work you do, for it is all necessary. I cannot stress this enough. For those who work daily from their homes for the common good, they will be exalted by the Heavens. There is a time and place for everything. Both solo and group work are necessary for those serious Lightbearers that are needed, every single one of them.*

*This is why I had you "gather around this campfire" as I wanted you to feel the communion of energies that are making and will make a supreme difference in your world. Everything you are reading here will grow in a richer, deeper understanding over time. This material is designed to support you in increasing ways. Together you will learn the ways of the spiritual warrior, the peaceful warrior, the strong and unstoppable warrior. You have been waiting for this invitation and it is here.*

(I was so caught up in channel I didn't realize until later how Michael created the perfect segue to the next chapter.)

# CHAPTER FIVE

## Invitation to the Sword

You have learned about the magical way that this book came to life, to understand its inception and just how blessed, validated, and vital this mission is. Michael's messages then came through providing a deeper perspective and understanding of the work before us, which you may revisit, at times. And now we move further into the purpose of this book and why it was written for you, for all of us.

Clearly, this book is more than a call for deeper awareness of what is occurring with our planet and all of life, it is a call for immediate action. As you can see, it is clearly directed from the Heavens, as represented by Archangel Michael, for us to understand and assume our new responsibility, that of being spiritual warriors. If you found your way to this book, you are most likely being called into action as a spiritual warrior—the peaceful, and yet determined and empowered warrior.

Michael's sword is the instrument of the warrior. Please know that the sword is the tool, the symbol, the way to work with and channel the Divine energies that pour through us when we use it. His sword will become an extension of each of us.

I hope that you, beautiful and powerful soul, join me and others in this mission to use Michael's sword, to bring Light, truth, and protection to yourself, your loved ones, and to the world. Maybe you have already been receiving signs and messages regarding this mission, even mirroring mine in some way. And, right now, perhaps you are hearing Michael's whispers or feel him around you, as you read these words.

**Archangel Michael is now inviting you, Divine Lightbearer, to pick up his sword.**

If you accept, please proclaim to Archangel Michael your acceptance of this mission. You will find the sword to be a gift that holds the greatest honor and power imaginable. As one of Archangel Michael's Warriors of Light, you will be working right alongside him.

Michael's sword has changed me forever and I believe it will change you too, in the best way possible. I am growing stronger. I am full of greater faith. I am in greater touch with the love within and outside of me. I feel more compassionate and understanding. I am empowered like never before, and no longer hold feelings of helplessness as I witness such chaos in the world! I have been clearly led to become an active warrior joined with the forces of Light, and Michael asks if this includes you. With my whole heart, I am so excited for you to join us in this mission. *This book will provide the information and guidance needed to learn to work with Michael's sword.*

I suggest that before you begin working with the sword, you see yourself aligned with the mightiest forces of Light in the Heavens, especially Archangel Michael. We can love and appreciate all that our angels do for us, and yet not see them as separate from and higher than us. However, we have been "conditioned" to see the separatism in everything, certainly with the Heavens, even for those of us fully aware of angelic presence all along.

So, while we may naturally separate ourselves in this way, we can proactively choose to become one with the angels. When we do so, we set our relationships with them on a much higher plane. We open up to much more to treasure. Just as we are growing our understanding of just how truly connected we all are to each other, the Earth, as one—the same is true with all beings, including those in Heaven.

It behooves us to claim our own magnificence as we lift ourselves from misbeliefs of being "not good enough," "unlovable," or whatever mindset(s) controls and runs us. Who we really are is love, each of us, just as the angels are. And of all the ways we reach for our Divine potential or qualities, Michael's sword can especially help lead us there.

As we move further on this continuum to great change on our Earth, our relationship to our angels will grow, eventually, in ways beyond our imaginations right now. And as we embrace the sword with Archangel Michael, this is the ultimate example! As a channel and representative of him, I can honestly tell you I never could have imagined myself in this role. But what I found was that it came naturally, as if I've done this many times before. You, too, may feel you've been participating in a dress rehearsal for this mission, throughout your life and, perhaps, even your past lives.

Here is what Michael has to say about growing our connection to our angels and no longer seeing them as separate from us. It came directly from my E-course "A Month with Michael and Mary."

*The relationship between angel and human is a sacred one. It is a Divine communion of energies coming together for the sake of spiritual advancement, support, and for evolutionary purposes. Practice thinking of your angelic support team in this way, and, yes, elevate yourself to this level, human angel, for these bonds, this perspective, will help you grow your own wings and your way of seeing yourself as a high being of Light. Thinking of yourself as separate and of lower vibrations is the old way, the way of a soon to be obsolete past. Treat us as you do your friend; laugh with us, bring us into your conversations, your thoughts, your activities, and your dreams. And there you will create relationships that will always serve and never take away or drain. The angels are here for you, always.*

This was channeled years ago, well before I embraced the magnificence of Michael's sword, when he would actually ask us to utilize this tool to help shift our world. And yes, this is indeed a Divine communion of energies coming together for the sake of spiritual advancement, support, and for evolutionary purposes—especially for evolutionary purposes.

What are some ways you can commune with the angels, if you aren't already doing so?

- Greet them as you wake each morning
- Laugh with them
- Ask them for help with anything you wish
- Know they are always there for you
- Speak to them, as casually as you would a friend (as you can see, I usually refer to Archangel Michael as simply "Michael")
- Share in the joy when something wonderful happens, and imagine them smiling and celebrating, because they are!
- Ask them for a sign
- Request they hold your hand or touch your face (you may feel a tingling energy sensation, and they may even gently move your head)
- Always know you deserve this connection
- Touch base with anything you wish to share upon wakening and before going to sleep

It is most vital to always know who you are connecting with, intending only those of the Light. As you connect in a deeper way with your angels, especially with Archangel Michael, you will find your connection with the sword grow, as well. Michael just gave me the image of the olive branch. As we know, the olive branch is the recognized symbol of peace. *The sword is ultimately the way to peace as we claim our peaceful spiritual warrior way*, he says just now.

Note: As I edit this chapter on 11/22/17, I am surprised by yet another synchronicity. Upon waking this morning and realizing the date, as I love master numbers, I then had the sad remembrance of this day as well, when John F. Kennedy was assassinated in 1963. Later this morning, I posted a preview quote from this book onto my Facebook page and was struck by the irony of someone else's post mentioning that JFK extended olive branches around the world.

I felt to search on the Internet "JFK + olive branch" and was led to a revealing article on www.content.time.com by David Talbot, on June 21, 2007, called "John F. Kennedy: Warrior for Peace." Is this not what this book is about, Warriors for Peace? David writes: "Young Jack Kennedy developed a deep, visceral disgust for war because of his—and his family's—experiences in it. 'All war is stupid,' he wrote..."

It appears that those of us who despise war the most are being called into spiritual battle. And I have goosebumps now as I hadn't even thought of the connection of King Arthur's Camelot to our former president. *Camelot*, having been JFK's favorite musical, later became the reference nickname to his administration after his passing! As the article states: "Immediately after John F. Kennedy's death, he was wrapped in gauzy myths of Arthurian gallantry."

In the next chapter, we will begin working with the sword. It's a very personal process as you work with Michael; this book is a guide. I look forward to learning of others' ways of seeing and working with his sword. Ever since the awareness of Michael's sword became front and center in my life, I have shared this understanding with those closest to me.

When writing my daughter about the sword, she saw the sword similarly as crystal light but articulated it in such a way that touched me deeply. I knew that her profoundly wise and intuitive interpretation was meant to be included here.

"Since swords are heavy, I'm imagining it being extremely clear and made of diamond, and really, really light (in all ways, weight, radiance, and energy), and using it like an extension of my arm. When I tune into its essence, it feels very, very powerful—almost like just thinking about it erases the shadows in my mind, amazing! I hold it and swing it around in my mind's eye, but even just imagining it near me, touching me, feels oddly protective in itself, you know?"

She added, "When I think of diamonds, I think of our human selves. Diamonds are impervious to anything except themselves—just as it is only really our own selves that allow what affects us or not. While this reality we are currently in is a balance between divine path and will, I still feel like Michael's sword is more about will, as we have to choose to wield it—so that's why I find it fitting. It's not only about being one of the strongest materials on this planet, but about the 'weakness,' being its own self, and all about will and our own personal strength and power, you know?"

Karen was not yet aware of my referring to that special place at Moraine Lake as the Diamond Vortex. Also, we had not talked about free will in this context, and yet she seemed to immediately understand it all. Everything was coming together to prepare for this invitation to you, thanks to angels and human angels.

# CHAPTER SIX

# Working with the Sword

Let me begin this chapter with the reminder, for those who may skip around the book, that Archangel Michael's sword will not hold any power in the hands of those wishing to do harm. It will be an impossible feat as this most powerful Archangel, who sees and knows all, decides who can use his sword. As mentioned earlier, not only will the sword not work with ill intent, but he made clear that the mere intention to use his sword in this manner will result in karmic retribution ten times over.

Lightbearers feeling called to this mission from their hearts, who are desiring to spread Light over the untruths, the deceptions, the darkness—to transcend what no longer serves—have been invited to use the sword. We will go step by step learning how to prepare for and use the sword, as one of Archangel Michael's Warriors of Light! The following is a guideline. *Please follow your intuition, your heart, for your own process that will lead to the same result: channeling Divine Light, Archangel Michael, and your higher self as a triune melding of energies—emitted through you and out the sword.*

Step One: FIND A SWORD. First, seek a tangible item to hold to symbolize at least the handle of Michael's sword. This can be a crystal, a rock, a gem—even an actual sword if you wish. I initially desired a sword, but soon realized I wanted something to easily wield, nothing too heavy or cumbersome. I see Michael's sword as weightless as it is of Light, and thus I prefer to hold something small, or at least light, and then visualize the rest. Although I do know I will manifest a true sword at some point, as may you. Perhaps you can use or even whittle a piece of wood and make your own. *Or, you can use your own creative imagination without holding anything in the physical—your arm can be the sword with the energy emanating out your hand!* It's up to you. We are all different. Find your way and make it your own.

Step Two: PICK UP THE SWORD. See Archangel Michael placing the sword in the "ground" before you, handle up. (After he has offered the sword to you the first time, you can always just pick up the sword. Again, it is up to you.) See the precious gift and feel its energy. Now, pick up your sword (your tangible representation, if you have one) and put your hand(s) holding the sword right to up to your forehead—your hand(s) over your third eye—imagining the length of the sword pointing upward, toward the Heavens.

Step Three: CALL FORTH ARCHANGEL MICHAEL AND THE LIGHT. Literally call for Michael and *know* that he is there, instantly. Feel him with you. You will soon breathe in Liquid Light from the New Sun through the crown of your head. The New Sun is only new to us. It is the spiritual sun beyond the sun that we know. It is also known as the Great Central Sun, and the Light it emanates is responsible for our evolution. *I recommend strong and audible deep breaths to assertively bring forth the Light energy, hand(s) still at your third eye.*

With at least three deep breaths, breathe in Liquid Light through your crown, melded with Archangel Michael's and your Higher Self's energy— a trinity of energy—into your physical body as you elevate your human self. Your whole body will fill with this Light of liquid that flows effortlessly through every cell and fiber of your being. Just stay with this until you fully own and feel the power of your role and your ability to perform. Note: Steps One through Three can take a matter of just seconds with practice, faith, and trust.

If you find it difficult to bring forth these energies, or wish for assistance, ask Michael to help you in what will become a natural process, as you simply focus on Light and this triune of energies.

Step Four: CONNECT TO YOUR HEART. Move your hand holding the sword from third eye to in front of your heart chakra, with the sword still pointing upwards. As you take slower, softer breaths in and out, connect to love, feeling the immense power of love in your heart now. Be sure that it is detached love, without specific thoughts of anyone or thing or situation. Just feel the bliss and enjoy being in that space as long as you need before proceeding. You may feel it from your head down to your toes, or perhaps concentrated in one area. As Michael said earlier: *You must raise your frequency to own the whole of your powerful self.* Whether it comes with the first try or after several tries, it does not matter—it will all become a natural process. Once you feel the bliss, you are ready for the next step.

Step Five: RAISE THE SWORD. With practice, or perhaps immediately, you will feel an electrical pulsing or tingling energy flowing from your arm(s), hand(s) and/or fingertips. The intensity level may range from quite subtle to strong, and it could vary each time. Allow your heart to tell you what to raise the sword to, for Light, Truth, and Protection. If you have things weighing on you, weighing on your heart, weighing on your energy in your personal life—please address these first. Use the sword to illuminate and transmute energies in your personal life first, and you will be more empowered and stronger to take action on behalf of the Earth for more worldly issues.

*Using your imagination, be wherever the energy is being sent,* unless you are able to be right there in person, and with Michael by your side. It is all intention. So, if the intended issue is in another part of the world, imagine yourself there. As Michael said, on some level you will be there. If it is in the skies, raise yourself holding the sword and with Michael by your side as you channel Divine energy through you and out the sword. *I make it a daily practice to send myself way out in space, wielding the sword over and around the whole Earth, again and again—for Light, truth, and protection the whole world over.*

Raise the sword that is beaming love and Light, pouring like liquid outward, with detachment from any emotion but neutral love. Detach from any thoughts of darkness as you raise the sword—stay above the situation and focus only on the Light itself. Neutrality is crucial and a practiced trait.

One of the ways I focus on the task, and without allowing any emotional attachment to it, is by repeatedly speaking and feeling the words "For Light, truth, and protection," again and again if I need to, while seeing the issue from a high and Divine perspective. I imagine seeing it as Archangel Michael would see it. As you do this, feel and deeply embrace the truth that Light has power over the dark. *Where the Light shines, no darkness can remain—so trust the Light to do the work, and with gratitude.*

See the Light coming through and out the full length of your sword, in your imagination. Wield the sword if you wish, perhaps making circular or sideways figure eight (infinity) movements. If protecting myself, I repeatedly circle the sword over my head pointing down, clearing out any unwanted energies. Move your body or stay still as you hold the sword—do whatever you feel moved to do without pushing it—just go with it and *let the Light do its job*. And then, return the sword to placement of hand over your third eye when you feel the sword work is complete.

It cannot be stated strongly enough to raise the sword with neutrality. This is intense or focused neutrality, as Michael stated he cannot use the sword without intensity, and neither can we. But it is not to be used with anger, hatred, or judgment. Please feel the difference. The intensity, or focus, is the drive for change as a Warrior of Light. When we work together with Michael, he can help us maintain that higher perspective.

How does this feel to you? Can you already feel that by doing this work, bringing this energy through you on a daily basis, it will benefit you and your energy field significantly? As you work with the sword, take note of how things shift, within you and outside of you. As you continue to use the sword, you will experience shifts that will grow your confidence in the sword and desire to work with it more and more. You may wish to journal your experiences. Once this book is published, I will create a platform for people to gather, share experiences and successes, and grow our sword work together via www.michaelsswordandyou.com.

When working with the sword, it takes a great deal of energy especially when addressing several issues in one period of time. Therefore, it is important to take sufficient breaks and refuel by resting, listening to music, incorporating movement, infusing humor and play in your life with loved ones, and/or, ideally, getting out in nature.

You may at times hear a whisper from Michael to raise the sword on something. Oftentimes, there will be a feeling within to raise the sword—an unmistakable urge. As Michael shared, your heart, your soul, will be in the captain's seat.

Important: Do not direct the sword right at anyone. If you are protecting yourself from someone's energy, for instance, you can hold the sword pointing upwards and between the two of you.

When you wake in the morning, a great way to start each day is to raise the sword for you, and perhaps before going to sleep, as well. Simply go through the steps above and use the sword to cut any energetic cords, wielding the sword down and around your aura intending full protection, warding off anything that does not serve you. And, of course, any time you feel a pull on your energy field, unexplained sudden exhaustion, or thoughts and feelings that are not yours, just raise and wield the sword around you, casting out potential unwanted energies or influences.

Shield or no shield, you may be asking. I never thought to have a shield because Archangel Michael *is* my shield, he is my protector, as he is yours! You are welcome to provide any shielding you feel necessary, though; this is just my choice and way. If at any time I feel interfered with or attacked psychically, I obviously call on Michael and use the sword. But I also have a practice of drawing on my own inner power and imagining myself covered in squares of impenetrable steel and on the outside of each square is a mirror. So, whatever someone tries to send me is mirrored right back.

Here is a list of possible areas we can use the sword to illuminate and cut to the truth and transmute, within and around us, in our personal lives.

1) Our Physical/Mental/Emotional/Spiritual States
2) Our Inability to Forgive Self or Others
3) Our Conditional Love
4) Our Fears
5) Our Confusion
6) Our Shadow Side
7) Our Conditioning
8) Our Anxieties and Worries
9) Our Apathy, Despair, or Depression
10) Our Relationship Challenges, Hurts, Betrayals
11) Our Protection from Dark Entities
12) Energetic Cords Sent from Others or We Send to Others
13) Our Misbeliefs; Unlovable, Not Good Enough
14) Our Lack of Self-Esteem
15) Our Lack of Abundance
16) Our Health Issues
17) Our Weaknesses
18) Our Stuckness
19) Our Mistrust
20) Our Anger
21) Our Addictions
22) Our Jealousies
23) Our Judgments
24) Our Cognitive Dissonance
25) Our Resistance to Necessary Change
26) And Whatever Else May Come Up

After you feel you have addressed the self, you are ready to address planetary issues. I suggest we work as often as possible on what many of us believe is the most significant issue plaguing our beautiful planet and all of life on Earth: geoengineering or climate engineering. And then, perhaps our food. We must know and *believe* we have the power to shift this world, as well as our own personal lives. The world needs us now. The sooner we can address the darkest of the dark plaguing our world, the better.

We can use the sword to illuminate and transmute the darkness on some of the greatest challenges of our time that are endangering our planet and all that reside on it.

Here is a list of issues that are constantly addressed by truthers. *Even if you deem these as falsities or "conspiracy theories," it cannot hurt to raise the sword of Light to them to bring forth whatever the truth is, right? You are spreading Light and that is a most excellent choice of action on literally anything.* You may choose to heavily focus on those things you feel most passionate about, or you may work with most or all of these. You cannot go wrong when you follow your heart's guidance. Of course, while this list is a good start, it is absolutely incomplete. So please add to it as you deem fit on these pages or you may wish to make your own list.

1) Geoengineering/Climate Engineering *
2) Poisoned Foods with GMOs, Pesticides, etc.
3) Poisoned Water with Flouride, etc.
4) Fracking
5) Illuminati
6) Vaccinations

7) The War Machine

8) The Cancer Machine

9) The Pharmaceutical Machine

10) The Medical and Insurance Industries

11) Suppression of Cures to Diseases

12) Suppression of Inventions

13) Mainstream News

14) The Puppet Political Leaders

15) The Controllers Behind the Political Leaders

16) Fukushima Cover-up/Nuclear Plant Dangers

17) Corporations Taking Over

18) Banks Taking Over

19) Rigged Elections

20) The Dark Side of Money

21) Washington D.C.

22) The Vatican

23) London and "Royalty"

24) Famine

25) Agenda 21

26) 911 Cover-up

27) Federal Reserve

28) Fraudulent Governmental Agencies

29) JFK Cover-up and many others

30) Mysterious "Suicides" of Truthers,
    Alternative Health Practitioners, etc.

31) Las Vegas Shooting Cover-Up and others

32) California and Other "Wildfires" Cover-up

33) Failing Education System

34) Abused AI (Artificial Intelligence)
    Technology

35) Programming/Brainwashing of Children

36) Programming/Brainwashing of Adults

37) Hiding and Distortion of Sacred Knowledge

38) Dark, hidden use of Sacred Symbols, Names Numbers, Geometry in Mass Culture
39) Standing Rock and All Pipeline Disasters
40) Extreme Weather Manipulation & HAARP
41) The Georgia Guidestones
42) Project Blue Beam
43) Brainwashing through Religion
44) Simply all Greed
45) Simply all Corruption
46) Simply all War
47) Pedophilia
48) Pornography Using Children
49) Sex Trafficking & Human Trafficking
50) Animal Cruelty in the Wild, in Farming Practices, & Domesticated
51) False Flags
52) Laser Weapons that Cause "Forest Fires" and other Destruction
53) Deforestation
54) Militarized Policing
55) Underground Cities
56) Failing Infrastructure
57) Rampant Big Brother Behavior Everywhere
58) Indoctrination of Men, Women, and Children
59) Suppression of Wealth for the Majority
60) Racism, Sexism, all Discrimination
61) Mind Control/Remote Viewing/Psychic Attack
62) Invisible Pollutants, Wifi Radiation
63) Smart Meters
64) EMF Exposure
65) Planned 5G
66) Planned RIFD Chipping Humans
67) Slave Labor

68) Violent Extraction of Oil, Gas, Timber and Minerals
69) Gross Manipulations and Deceptions of Consumers for Profit
70) Net Neutrality Fight
71) Humanity's Enslavement
72) Plastic and Waste Crisis
73) All We Don't Know About
74) And Many More We Do, But Not Listed...
* <u>most significant, please address daily among</u> <u>all others you choose to focus on</u>

Protect your precious mind and, again, detach emotionally. Not easy! Insanity and the extreme darkness are quite impossible to understand, so let's put our energies on transmutation and casting away of all that does not serve life and our planet.

Areas we can direct the sword for healing and transmutation of hurting places on our Earth.
1) The Whole Earth
2) The Atmosphere, Biosphere
3) The Melting Ice Caps
4) The Oceans and Dying Coral, Plastic, Radiation, and Oil Spill Pollution
5) The Lakes, Rivers, Drinking Water, Poisoned by Fracking, Oil Spills, Flouride Additives
6) World Hunger
7) Overpopulation Ramifications
8) Floods to Droughts
9) Crops Contaminated with GMOs, Pesticides, and Chemtrail Fallout
10) Our Vital Bees and Other Endangered and Extinct Insect Species

11) Animals and Marine Life Suffering, Pillaged, Endangered, or Facing Extinction
12) Plants/Trees Endangered or Facing Extinction
13) Soil Contaminated with Chemtrail Fallout, GMOs, Pesticides, Oil Leaks (Standing Rock and many others)
14) Humans Contaminated and Endangered from all the Above and More
15) Human Health Declining
16) Body/Mind/Spirit Imbalances
17) The Educational System, Kids "Dumbed Down" and Programmed
18) Adults "Dumbed Down," Becoming Apathetic, Indifferent, Programmed via Mass Media
19) Awakening Consciousness, in General
20) Our Pineal Glands Calcified from Flouride
21) The Hungry, the Poor, the Sick, the Homeless
22) The Lonely, the Depressed
23) The Abused and Neglected
24) The Physically, Mentally, Emotionally Challenged
25) The Refugees
26) The Confused
27) The Hopeless
28) All We Don't Know About
29) And Many More We Do, But Not Listed...

The Heavens are celebrating you for your commitment as a Warrior of Light!

Please pay attention to personal messages of guidance and revealing synchronicities—often sent from Michael—that occur in conjunction with reading this book and performing your sword work. This will help you maintain your exuberant efforts in this mission, bar none.

************

Feel free to add to your lists here:

# CHAPTER SEVEN

# The Big Eye

I have always been drawn to eyes. I used to draw them often and with particular detail in my younger years. Even as a child, I feel I somehow knew they were the windows to our souls. I always felt best connected with a loved one, a friend, or even a stranger through the eyes. We all have our insecurities but direct eye contact isn't one of mine. I always felt there was something more to this connection, and it was an extraordinary and unexpected unfolding over decades of time.

The single eye has served as a prevalent and synchronistic message to me, personally, since 2001—six years after experiencing that Divine white

Light in my right eye which marked the start of my conscious spiritual journey. I share the following remarkable stories in *I Can See Clearly Now*:

Sometimes signs are purely an unfolding. You may need days, weeks, months, or even years to fully understand what they mean, and, thus, patience is required. They are a peek into the future with a display of a potential occurrence, path, or understanding. An absolutely stunning thread of synchronicities is still unfolding in my life.

On January 10, 2001, I decided to treat myself with a visit to a bookstore. I bought a novel called *The Saving Graces*[5]. I hadn't read anything but spiritual publications for years but felt strangely compelled to purchase this book. After leaving the store, I drove to "Old Town" for some authentic southwestern food. Old Town is located not far from what New Mexicans call "The Big I," where the state's main expressways, I-40 and I-25, intersect. At that time, this intersection was undergoing a major renovation.

Following a quick meal, I headed for home, merging onto the expressway to go eastbound on I-40 toward The Big I. My car started to sound strange. I kept pushing on the gas pedal but could not achieve a steady rate of acceleration, and I suddenly realized what was happening. For the first time in my life, I was running out of gas, with nowhere to go. Because of the major road reconstruction, cement barricades lined the

---

[5] Gaffney, Patricia. *The Saving Graces*. New York: Harpertorch, 1999.

lanes, which prevented the shoulder from "saving" me.

I thanked God out loud when I saw an exit about an eighth of a mile down. There was a gas station ahead, and I would be just able to sputter my way to the exit. However, the exit ramp was barricaded as well. I started praying very hard and very loudly; my car moved incrementally with every few pushes on the gas pedal while cars and semis rushed past me.

Although my car seemed to be running on fumes at this point, I somehow made it safely to where the shoulder reopens for the southbound approach onto I-25, right at the main intersection—The Big I. While intensely thanking God for keeping me safe, I put my car into park. At that moment, a truck with a huge picture of Christ on the cross went past me. A truck with a picture of Christ on it? I couldn't believe this but had no time to think about it, because suddenly several horns started to sound, and I heard brakes screeching behind me.

Was I going to get hit? What was going on now? I looked in my side-view mirror and could not believe my eyes. A little Chihuahua was running along the same path I'd just driven toward The Big I! Here was this tiny dog right in the midst of the biggest interchange in all of New Mexico. Terrified, it was desperately trying to find safety as drivers slammed on their brakes to avoid hitting it.

I immediately got out of my car to save it, as it ran toward where I was parked. Being so scared it didn't realize I was trying to help it, and to my horror, it started to go into the road. I immediately grabbed it, and at that moment, it bit me out of fear. During this time, I was vaguely aware that a police car had been parked about one hundred feet or so ahead of me. The officers just sat in the car while I played hero, but I later realized that I was the one who needed to save this little Chihuahua.

With feelings of great relief, I took the dog over to the policemen, showed them that it had no tag, and then offered to take it to the animal shelter. They wanted to take it themselves, but it was hard for me to let them. I felt a connection to this tiny white, brown, and black being that somehow survived The Big I. How on earth did a little dog like this get onto the expressway? I wanted to be sure it would be okay after all it had endured. (As it turned out, it was quarantined for a few days, and on the morning that it was to be put up for adoption, it was selected and taken just ten minutes after the shelter opened.)

After the policemen took the Chihuahua, I called AAA, and they came with a gallon of gas. I wanted to fill up right away, vowing to never again drive on a sparsely filled tank, and went to a nearby gas station. I pumped some gas and then called my husband, on my cell phone, to tell him what had happened.

As I drove down a side street, explaining to Jack the astonishing occurrence with the Chihuahua, *another* Chihuahua walked right in front of my car! I was screaming into the phone, telling Jack about this light brown Chihuahua that just crossed the street directly in front of me. Aren't they lapdogs, people dogs, which are rarely outside on their own and certainly never far from their owners?

I'm sure my poor husband's ears did not appreciate my screams of shock. He, being used to my synchronistic experiences and my yearning to find meanings in each of them said playfully, "I think it means you need to go to Taco Bell." He was referring to the Taco Bell commercials that featured their popular Chihuahua mascot. I knew that the message here was much more significant than that. The Universe had gone through a lot of trouble to synchronize these amazing events. What I didn't know then was that this was just the beginning and that the meaning of these events would unfold over several years.

The synchronicities continued through the day. I began reading *The Saving Graces*—the book I had bought that morning. The first chapter described how four women friends *save a dog!*

Yes, clearly the Universe was up to something. In this chapter, I will share several stunning examples of similar messages, including this one told in the same chapter which rivaled and yet perfectly mirrored the Big I experience:

We lived in the desert, which consisted mostly of dirt, rocks, junipers, and cacti, in an area with homes that were separated by at least an acre. Situated in the foothills of the Sandia Mountains, the area was very hilly, and our mailbox was a half mile from our house. One day, my young son asked to make the climb up, between the homes, to the mailbox. He had never hiked to the mailbox before. Being the ever-protective mom, and because we did live among snakes and other wonders, I asked him to take his walkie-talkie along.

At one point in his journey, he used his walkie-talkie to tell me that he'd found some mail. It hadn't been in the mailbox; he'd found it lying in the dirt between two homes halfway up. I told him to bring it home and that we'd get it to the right person. When he returned, I saw that there was no address on the envelope, only the name "Larry," and it appeared to contain a greeting card. It looked as if it had been on the ground for months, soaked with rain, and then dried; it was quite warped but still sealed.

I didn't know of a man named Larry. Given that winds sometimes surpass fifty miles per hour in our area, the envelope could have been blown a great distance. I called several neighbors to ask if they knew of a Larry, but no one did either. One woman told me to open the envelope, because the contents may provide a clue. So with my kids there, I opened it. Indeed, it was a greeting card.

On the front of it was a picture of a Chihuahua. Above the dog was an image of an eyeball—a very strange-looking card. It was my very wise and intuitive seven-year-old daughter, Karen, who figured it out right away: "Mom, it's a big eye! You know, the Chihuahua and The Big I!" *Wow.* Can you imagine how we felt as we looked at the picture and began to understand? We couldn't believe it. Inside the card were the words "Ay, Chihuahua! You're how old?" It was a birthday card (see photo). To top it off, it was signed by "Scott," the name of my son. And here it was Scott, himself, who suddenly desired to hike this path which led him to finding the card with a miraculous message. All three of us hugged each other; always celebrating these incredible occurrences.

Fast forward a dozen years later, I began "gazing" in the summer of 2013, a practice where I channel Divine energy through my eyes to people both in live audiences and remotely via pictures. People have had extremely varied and powerful responses to the energy as you can see on my testimonial page at www.newsungazing.com. I always gaze with the presence of Archangel Michael, Mary Magdalene, Jesus, and Mother Mary. Time and time again, those receiving the gaze in person would see me morph into these very beings, or feel their presence, and usually without knowing that they are a part of my team. So that proved extremely validating.

The eyes have it, everything was about the eyes and synchronicity continually validated this! As seen in *Look Up!*, this cloud was quite miraculous:

When you look really closely, you may spot several beings in this image, particularly on the right side of the photo and however subtle. But what I want to point out most especially can be seen above the sun. Do you, too, see a very realistic eye? Simply look for the darkest part of the upper left quadrant of the photo, which is the pupil of an eye. To the right of it (a bit hard to see) is another much smaller eye, approximately a quarter of the size of the large eye. There have been many occasions I look up and see eyes looking back at me ever since I began my gazing work, where I channel Divine energy through my eyes (www.newsungazing.com). I captured these particular eyes in the sky just one month after I began my new work in August of 2013.

Just this morning, on November 8, 2017, I was somehow led to the image of the promotional poster of the animated movie *The Prophet* and noticed something I hadn't before. Directly above the movie's title is an open hand facing the viewer with a single big eye in the center of the palm. I then recalled when a couple of people reported they saw the celestial "Eye of God" before me as I gazed at them. Why were they seeing the Helix Nebula hundreds of light years away while locked in a gaze with me? Clearly, Michael synchronistically led me to this sighting and these thoughts because, as I knew, I needed to write a chapter in this book to further consider the message of The Big Eye.

Yes, it was time to delve deeper than ever into the meaning of the all-seeing eye, a symbol following me around for nearly seventeen years. I knew it was a most powerful symbol of God, and yet, as many of us know, it has been used by the dark side, just as they use other sacred symbols, names, numbers, and geometry—and that includes the pyramid. As you probably are well aware of, on the back of an American dollar bill, a Federal Reserve Note, is a pyramid with an all-seeing eye at the top, separated from the rest of the pyramid. I simply searched on the Internet "all-seeing eye" just now and the first link I open is titled: "The All-Seeing Eye: Sacred Origins of a Hijacked Symbol." How perfect a find.

As seen on www.consciousreporter.com, an article written by David Percival and posted on June 17, 2014, poses the question: "Is the all-seeing eye a symbol of divine omniscience or sinister influence? Today it symbolizes control and domination by a shadowy elite, but its original use was quite different. This article traces its use and meaning back to ancient times, when it was a symbol of divine providence, powerfully representing spiritual truth and awakening."

Subtitled "Humanity is Losing Its Precious Symbology," this piece goes on to describe the eyes of Shiva, Buddha, Osiris, and the particularly familiar Eye of Horus, which symbolizes the third eye. "Horus being a sun god and symbolic of the universal Christ, a spiritual force which a suitably prepared person can merge with."

Next, I see a picture of a symbol of an eye in the palm of hand, Hamsa. It's the very same symbol I saw earlier today in "The Prophet" movie poster! The article goes on to say "A more Christian-themed representation of the Hamsa is an art work called 'The Divine World' by Kahlil Gibran." It's hard to believe that the first article I pull up refers to the magnificent author of *The Prophet*[6] and his artwork! Hamsa is known to ward off the "evil eye."

How remarkable is it that Michael clearly guided this whole day, to really delve into the Eye of God symbolism, which quickly validates ways that the sacred has indeed been hijacked? David continues: "The all-seeing eye is a powerful esoteric symbol which is widely misunderstood and misused today; few know what it originally stood for. It was originally symbolic of a higher spiritual power or God, a watchful caretaker of humanity or an awakened spiritual part within. But these days it has quite different associations."

David goes on to write: "Today the all-seeing eye is more likely to be seen as an 'Illuminati' symbol of control and surveillance by elites who to a large degree run the show on this planet at this time. This is because, over time, dark sinister forces have taken over esoteric symbols that for thousands of years were used to convey positive, helpful, uplifting spiritual messages and principles. The all-seeing eye is a prime example of how spiritual symbols have been hijacked and inverted. There has not really been much push to understand the symbol's original meaning or to reclaim it for the spiritual significance it first conveyed."

Well I, for one, am pushing for understanding and reclamation of this Divine symbol now, and with gratitude for the find of your fabulous article, David! At this point, I was on the edge of my seat in awe. Because earlier this day, I claimed that I'm going to help shift the way the all-seeing eye of God is

---

[6] Gibran, Kahlil, *The Prophet*. New York: Alfred A. Knopf, 1923.

represented, in ways that I can, not only via this chapter, but by displaying a representation of the single eye on the cover of this book. The eye is behind the sword and within the diamond shape overseeing *above* and *below*. It feels so auspiciously planned from the Heavens, effortlessly unfolding before me.

Here I am reading the words in this article that mirrored what I felt so strongly must be done just hours earlier! We simply must shift all of the dark manipulations and restore the sacred in our symbols, names, numbers, geometry, etc. It is something we must raise the sword to.

When I scrolled down to the comment section of this article, my eyes widened. A person wrote "Throughout my entire childhood to teenage years up until now I always draw the same eye whenever I have a pen and paper in hand." I honestly wrote this chapter in order. I described my desire to draw eyes since my younger years first thing this morning, found the article, and then just read this comment now as I write this. I'm sharing all these synchronicities to show you I cannot have any doubt about any of this. It has all been laid out magically for this mission and thus yours, if you, too, have chosen to accept this calling.

Note: Just prior to this book going into production, Michael guided me to "Leave now," to take a walk by Standley Lake, on January 4, 2018. The last time he asked me to do so was when I came across the green glass egg (seen on page 99). Well this time, I saw this rock that not only looks like a hand, but Hamsa! Not only that, but this lady said to me, "By the way, there

148

are two coyotes ahead." Just before leaving for this walk, my daughter messaged me that she and my son saw two coyotes when out last night.

I searched on the Internet the spiritual meaning of the coyote. I *heard* to open the third link listed and was shocked by the subhead on www.universeofsymbolism.com... Merlin!

## Coyote Symbolism ~&~ Meaning

"the magic of Merlin
awaits you"

I must also share that alongside this challenging year, I have also been blessed with a huge resurgence of synchronicities regarding The Big Eye, and yes, even Chihuahuas. Miracles and mayhem can exist side by side, and help us to persevere no matter what we are faced with.

When I was visiting Santa Fe after my extensive travels and just prior to the start of 2017, my friend Mia who lives on the other side of the world and who created the call to "Magnum," wrote me that she sees *a Big Eye watching me*. Mia is a most gifted channel who often surprises me with simple and yet profound gems such as this.

With her powerful message, I asked Mia if she remembered that reference to The Big Eye in *I Can See Clearly Now*. She said she completely forgot, but yet clearly saw this. Within 24 hours of her message, I see this in Santa Fe, a store I hadn't seen before and with single eyes all around it!

150

A couple of weeks later, I was looking for a place to live in Santa Fe, temporarily. One morning on Craigslist, I saw a domed adobe-styled home available for rent in Taos. While I hadn't at all planned on living in Taos, about 90 minutes away, something told me to check out this place. I quickly researched to make sure that the town had an organic food store—just in case I was indeed meant to live there—and then set off to see the home.

The day proved synchronistic in so many ways. I quickly signed on the dotted line and found myself soon moving into what looked like a Big Eye, this little, unique dome home. What was also striking, was that the main window formed a huge triangle as you can see in the picture. On the other side was a passive solar triangular "window," which you can see in the reflection on the main window. Was this not reflecting The Big Eye with triangle symbolism?

I rented a U-Haul truck and drove all the belongings from my storage unit in Flagstaff to Taos, with car in tow. When I drove under the Big-I in Albuquerque, where the Chihuahua and the "Big Eye" miracle took place sixteen years prior, yet another miracle occurred.

Just when I was exactly under the very center of this huge expressway interchange, and as I ceremoniously recalled the extraordinary memory, I heard the phrase "Amazing Grace," repetitively, about seven times! It was a radio advertisement, and two words couldn't have been more fitting in that moment. *Saving Grace* was the title of the book I bought that morning, if you recall. Here I was making a full circle move back to New Mexico (I had moved there with my family in 1999) where the Chihuahua and Big Eye synchronicities began, and a resurgence of these signs was directly ahead.

All I needed was a Chihuahua, which I did get a couple of months later! I named her Grace. I found her hours away from where I lived, and was drawn to her like a magnet. She had a black heart shape on her white furred hip and was born on Valentine's Day! But after several weeks, I could no longer stay where I was, following the intense sabotage from dark energies, and moved back to Colorado. Where I was going to stay temporarily couldn't have dogs, so I very sadly gave her up.

I was directly guided to do so. Michael even influenced matter to prove that I must adhere to this guidance. When playing fetch with Grace, in the kitchen with her toy, I threw it onto the floor and the toy absolutely vanished into thin air before my eyes. I never saw that toy again! On some level, I knew that I was only meant to be a foster mom to Grace. We healed each other, and she then lived with a fine family that had another dog.

The Big Eye was everywhere, especially during this time while in the dome home; in the clouds, in symbols, in pictures, and within messages from others. For instance, a few months after Mia told me she sees The Big Eye watching me, I drove by that same storefront in Santa Fe with all the single eyes painted on it. Just as I was in front of the store, I received three sound notifications in succession on my cell phone. They were all messages from Mia.

I was at my friend's office in Santa Fe that same day and saw an envelope with a hand drawn picture of a single eye next to his name.

This was just two nights after another friend messaged me from Ojo Caliente, New Mexico. "Ojo" meaning "eye" in Spanish, he randomly typed out "The 'Eye'!" with an eye emoticon. This was Bryan, who mirrored what was going on at Lake Louise.

# The "Eye"! 👁

A couple of months later, I had another extraordinary day of revealing signs in the same vein. On the way to Albuquerque, I saw a billboard of a Chihuahua with one eye!

Next, I was awed to see a circular cut out of a single eye just sitting there on the pavement at a gas station—so random! Then I stopped for lunch in Santa Fe, and *heard* to ask the waitress where she's originally from. "Chihuahua, Mexico," of course!

After having moved back to Colorado, I went with my family to a restaurant I had never been to. Above where I sat was this single big eye in a newly painted mural.

If all that weren't enough, over several months I would so often see a single eye in my third eye vision when meditating. When I get visions there, they fade in and out, one after another, extremely real with detail as if watching something on television. They last just seconds before going onto the next image. Clearly, The Big Eye was speaking to me and it seemed to all culminate in a grander under-standing as I write this very chapter.

After enduring the chaos and heart-wrenching situations for the majority of 2017, I look back in retrospect and I can see clearly now that I needed to experience all of it. The Big Eye was watching and all the clues and hurt and bliss and pain and signs and betrayal and miracles brought me in perfect readiness and alignment for this mission, and writing this book for my fellow Warriors of Light.

*Will you join me* in bringing back the sanctity of all that is sacred and Divine, including the all-seeing eye of God, by raising the sword for them?

May we unite with Archangel Michael to call on the full return of all that is sacred in our world. All the sacred knowledge, symbols, names, numbers, geometry, and more that have been manipulated, exploited, and defaced by the dark. This includes The Big Eye, the all-seeing eye of God.

Well, as you can see, I wasn't exaggerating when I wrote in *I Can See Clearly Now* that it can take years for a sign to unfold and thus patience is required. The Chihuahua and The Big Eye story was so incredibly profound and miraculous, I remember wanting immediate answers. Instead, I had a long and yet perfect wait of seventeen years. But who am I kidding? There is always more in this rapidly unveiling world, and I await and am ready to experience and address what is next. To those who join me on this mission of bringing all that is sacred back to the forefront, the Heavens are rejoicing in your honor.

**************

I learned that more needs to come through on this very subject, signaled by waking up to a very strong message on this morning, December 19, 2017. While in somewhat of a lucid state, which is when I usually see visions in my third eye, I was awed by what showed up, like nothing I've seen before. It was a scrolling of symbols; dozens of various vibrantly colored shapes. Many appeared triangular in nature and they looked somewhat Egyptian and even otherworldly. It was hard to decipher anything specific because the scrolling was quick, and the whole vision lasting only seconds. To the side of the symbols I clearly saw the words "Make Sense." I immediately felt there was more I must make sense of about our sacred symbols.

So, I began this day by simply searching the phrase "hijacked symbols." Once again, the very first link I opened was most revealing and relevant. At www.belsebuub.com is an article "Reclaiming the Spiritual Symbols That Have Been Hijacked and Used Against Us." The article is written by Angela Pritchard, who happens to be the co-author of *The Path of the Spiritual Sun*[7]—similar to my title *The New Sun* which is considered to be the spiritual sun, so synchronicity was definitely in play.

The article starts out: "Spiritual symbols are powerful. Beneath the veneer of social norms they are being used in a hidden war. Not only have dark forces propagated the symbols of black magic into millions of unsuspecting homes, but additionally many of the world's great spiritual symbols of light have been demonized."

Indeed, all of us have been constantly subjected to advertising, corporation logos, products, music and television entertainment, and more—and even wearing on our bodies (whether via clothes or tattoos permanently etched onto skin)—featuring symbology that has been slanted with darkness. And all while many of the receivers have no clue regarding the meanings and energy behind them. It is time to break these cycles and norms in our

---

[7] Pritchard, Angela. co-author *The Path of the Spiritual Sun.* Fremantle: Mystical Life Pub. Ltd., 2017.

largely unawakened, unaware society. Just corporation logos alone are filled with hidden symbolism (such as 666) on products we may purchase or view constantly.

"For thousands of years, forces of darkness have tasked themselves with the aim of destroying spirituality and suppressing consciousness. They have infiltrated and/or founded religious groups, organizations and schools (such as the Freemasons, the Catholic Church, etc.); have hijacked their spiritual texts, teachings, symbols and knowledge; and have then shut it away, distorted, destroyed, and suppressed it."

We simply cannot get away from it, for it runs so rampant with roots so deep into the past, *but we can be aware, make new choices when possible, and raise the sword which will affect the past, too.* This article also hits on something that begs consideration, the effect of dark usage of symbols in other dimensions. "Everything we can see around us, including ourselves, is multi-dimensional—it's just that we are usually only aware of the physical part. Like everything else, symbols that are drawn here are visible in other dimensions, and according to the symbol, can attract or repel other dimensional forces and beings." Surely, this is one of the reasons why I was directed to address this message further.

What exists outside of us isn't all angelic, so we need to consider what we allow into our lives and trust our intuition and heart to lead us into creating surroundings that are truly light-filled. Because as we know, everything carries energy. This article's sobering point is well taken that the dark forces' "promotion brings these symbols into millions of homes, even billions, around the world, where they attract forces and beings of darkness into the lives of unsuspecting people." I immediately think of the music world, in many cases, and their dark influence on our youth, most especially.

I refer to many of the dark Super Bowl half-time shows as an example of mass influence, as well as music award shows, that are filled with dark worshiping "entertainment," not only forced on unaware fans, but many are blindly idolizing and praising it all. There's the negative side of the music industry, in general, churning out albums filled with demeaning, disempowering, and perceptible yet also subliminal darkness that is destructive to society. May we put a halt to being used and abused via the distortion, confusion, and massive conditioning that darkness has created.

Here is a little clue that Angela describes: "One tell-tale way to pick a symbol of black magic is if it is a symbol of light but inverted." And adds "Because the nature of darkness is the inverse of light, it follows that dark symbols will be those of light inverted." She describes how the pentagram, a symbol of light and truth, has been hijacked with distortion. Included in the article is a picture of an extravagant stained glass window where Angela notes: "An upside down pentagram cleverly concealed in a Catholic Church in its highest place of worship where it brings down demonic forces." She also addresses the hijacking of the all-seeing eye, the pyramid, the cross, the swastika, and more.

"Because symbols of light have the power to attract the forces of light, they also have the power to banish the forces of darkness. Stigmatizing them strips away the ability for people to use symbols of light to defend themselves against evil forces. In this way, humanity is being both deceived and disempowered." These key statements define where our work comes in with Michael's sword, while bringing authentic sacred symbols into our lives.

May we raise the sword for awareness, transmutation, and transcendence of all sacred symbolism and all sacred knowledge. Let us shine the Light via the sword for it all to be revealed and returned back to their sacred origin and power, which will in turn empower humanity. Our return to our spiritual nature by Divine birthright is key in these times, absolutely essential.

When I received the gift of the labradorite, and this was before my trip to the Diamond Vortex, as soon as I saw it in that unique long diamond shape, it really struck me. I knew its purpose immediately, to serve as the sword's handle which I was looking for. But I had no idea of the unveiling of the diamond symbolism to come.

This led me to search on the Internet just now "what does the diamond symbol represent?" I do know that Native Americans connect the diamond to the symbol of a butterfly, which of course represents transformation. In an article "A Global and an Eternal Symbol," on www.eternalsymbols.com, it gets right to the point. "When the geometric shape of the rhombus appears, a significant change is installed within the consciousness of a human being; one that supersedes the limited ego-self of the human personality and acts for the benefit of all people." The diamond, or rhombus shape, is seen as two triangles, representing yin and yang. "Both (male and female sexes) need to surrender their Yang to the Yin aspect of self. As such the reason for being on Earth for humanity is to unveil the Yin aspect of self."

More validation surfaced: "Symbols, especially geometric symbols, emit a frequency that can evoke within the physical expression of a human being this innate ability to reconnect with the lost knowledge of Truth of mankind. The loss of this ability is directly connected to the imbalance within our inner beings between the Yin/Yang polarity and this imbalance has thus been reflected for eons of time into our outer world. The results hereof are seen throughout our world and the times have now come that mankind will awaken from this energetic 'sleep' and remembers the human task of restoring inner and outer balance, because we can!"

And finally, these powerful questions are posed, and perhaps suggests in part why I was led to the Diamond Vortex: "Is the rhomboid shape just a fancy shape that appears 'by incident' all over the globe? Is there no 'proof' that this symbol represents the ideal of achieving a change of consciousness towards the good for all? Does this pre-monotheistic symbol refer to an inner experience of the Divine that got lost with the arrival of patriarch dogmatic religions? And if so, how can we reconnect to that innate ability, our individual human heritage? Can we allow for the possibility that there is more to our earthly being than we 'think'?"

From my third eye visions, I realized I ultimately needed to not only further make the case for regaining our sacred symbols, but to "make sense" of the meaning of the Diamond Vortex. This is utterly stunning when I consider how everything was just presented before me, especially at Moraine Lake, and then with so much unveiling since.

The image for the cover of this book was clearly guided by Michael, well before I explored the meaning of the diamond shape. It provides unfolding symbolism with not only the single eye and Michael's sword, but as revealed through the upward and downward triangles at the Diamond Vortex. This made me think of *The Da Vinci Code* where it describes the symbol of the male as a point-up triangle (as in the phallus) and the female as a point-down triangle (as in the womb). The uniting of these shapes creates a hexagram, male and female fused into Divine union. Are we not rebalancing the Divine Masculine with the Divine Feminine energies emerging now, as the article described?

I just now asked for Archangel Michael's input regarding the diamond, and he says:

*You have been led further toward something you have been seeking for years, a more in-depth under-standing of symbols and how they have been used for good and evil. You recently even thought of the character of this movie that just came to mind, who is a symbolism expert. You have followed this path to a degree with synchronicity, a destined path for you. And I tell you, the diamond... the diamond... it is a symbol for you all to put special focus on now, to reverse the enslavement of humanity, the discrim-ination of so many, and to now come into your wholeness, power, and freedom... finally.*

The diamond is the backdrop for the watchful all-seeing Eye of God with Archangel Michael's sword. Everything is coming together with much more to unfold. May we connect to the essence of the diamond symbol, and take control of our destiny and come into balance. Surely, as we do so with Michael's guidance, there will be much more to uncover and dispense about reclaiming our sacred symbology through future revelations and calls to shift this.

Later this day, I prepared to have dinner while watching a movie on my computer. Just as I sat down, I looked out the window and saw a big eye in a cloud. I began watching the movie and just minutes into it, the college student's astronomy teacher asks him to look through the telescope—only to see the "Eye of God" nebula.

Two days later, I watched *The Da Vinci Code* again, as Michael was hinting to do so in his message, and since then. I even brought up the movie in this book, in Chapter Two. The movie starts out with the lead character Robert Langdon giving a lecture promoting his book *Symbols of the Sacred Feminine* in the beginning of the movie, posing the question "How do we penetrate years, centuries, of historical distortion to find original truth?" As Robert spoke the latter of these words, you see him in front of a huge screen of symbols, which immediately reminded me of my extravagant third eye vision.

The movie, as you may well know, is filled with all kinds of symbolism and highlights much of the deception and suppression over centuries of time of Mary Magdalene, especially, who many of us believe is known to represent the Divine Feminine—the emerging force behind our Divine destiny.

# CHAPTER EIGHT

# The Aware Warrior & Self-Care

This chapter is designed to help you stay healthy, centered, protected, sane, and mostly very aware through these chaotic, exciting, and unprecedented times. *Awareness is self-care.* Included are various things to consider, to boost a deeper awareness in your personal life, as well as for your sword work. *However, I present this as mere opinion, as a personal perspective,* and perhaps similar to yours too. *Your own research is necessary;* we all must research and avoid listening to and trusting mainstream sources, especially. There is plenty of truth out there, but we have to seek it during these times so that we make sound choices in all aspects of life. I realize I may be preaching to the choir.

This chapter is included just as importantly to highlight both the necessity and more in-depth consideration of where to raise the sword. While I must bring up some of the unappealing, we simply must face truths as spiritual warriors. *And then we can detach from the situations as we raise the sword with love—maintaining our high vibrations!* It is not enough to just raise the sword, we must do so with enough awareness and intention so we know where our focus must lie.

Michael adds: *The time has come for truth, and all must be unveiled and now. For the changes will come swift when enough raise awareness. If people do not speak out, imagine humanity stuck in a bottleneck, and then suddenly the truths will create an explosion of shocking information versus a gentler way which you are witnessing and participating in now. Humanity has the choice to learn the truths with more or less ease, sooner rather than later.*

Many are devoting their lives now to be truthers. For instance, in the medical field a doctor or nurse aware of dangers and deceptions in medicine, pharmaceuticals, and/or vaccinations may even leave the careers they worked so incredibly hard for in order to speak out. Seek these truthers, those who can back their findings with the necessary scientific evidence and experience—while tuning into your intuition.

Some are lay persons who are devoting their lives now to search for evidence, and taking on journalist type roles day in and day out spreading necessary awareness. They are also facing increasing censorship, so the more of us that speak out, the better the chance to get messages conveyed without interference and while curbing all the propaganda. While we are still subject to very dark influences in our world, nothing behooves us more than to be educated on what is true. "Knowledge is power," said Sir Francis Bacon. Let's seek the truth and act from that point forth.

**Physical, mental, emotional, and spiritual health:** We are finding that alternative medicine and therapies with proper nutrition is often the way to optimal health. While we of course need conventional medical services and certainly for our survival at times—and there's so very much to be grateful for—there is also much that must be considered, even avoided in conventional medicine. We must consider various testing and "cures" for disease that could actually create or hasten disease. We must raise the sword for the right to have awareness of and legal access to known natural cures being kept from us. We must absolutely be aware of what immunizations (especially increasing numbers of them on very young bodies), flu shots, and various pharmaceuticals pushed on so many are really made up of and their true effects on us.

The best thing we can do for our bodies is to have a truly healthy diet. Poor dietary intake is really being called out now as the cause of most diseases and physical suffering. We are what we eat, indeed. We continually hear from many sources the importance of having a more alkaline diet rather than a mostly acidic one. We can stop "band-aiding" and rather go right to the source, the cause of physical issues in so many cases.

We simply must avoid the world of pseudo-foods, preserved foods, poison additives, excessive sugars, as much as possible—and most especially gmos and pesticide laden produce which also finds its way into so much, via plants and animal feed! Then we can put a halt to this vicious cycle of failing health for us and our precious children. The growing popularity of vegetarianism and veganism, is speaking ever loudly now for many reasons. There are several excellent documentaries out there about our food crisis, an easy way to achieve understanding.

Speaking of our children, may it be a priority to do our research and be especially aware, becoming activists on behalf of these beautiful young souls, the future of our world. And many of them are actually profoundly stepping into young activist roles. These higher vibrational children being born in recent decades are the ones who are less attached to belief systems and can easily accept and adapt to changes—in diet in this case—perhaps, easier than adults.

May we help our children shift their diets over-all and while perhaps not popular eating choices quite yet, we can be models for them to embrace and be proud of eating healthy foods for their bodies. Whole foods are the best "fast foods." School lunches can be made at home unless you have found a rare school that offers healthy choices.

During this writing, I learned of the first school district in the US to serve all organic and non-gmo foods, in California's Sausalito Marin City District, and may this snowball from here. However, nothing is better than what can come from home, hopefully organic and non-gmo foods. Organic foods prices are lowering. Growing an organic vegetable garden for our healthiest sustenance (in addition to being a great family activity) is a great response to our food crisis.

I recall Michael's prophecy he made years ago as stated in *Michael's Clarion Call*, when discussing how foods of lower vibration will not be able to exist in the new energy. We are indeed starting to see this in some cases, but in other cases it's worse: *Yes, my dear, foods will change too. The dangerous additives, preservatives, antibiotics in meat, overdosing of sugar, and the list goes on and on, will no longer be tolerated by your bodies, or society itself. The truths about the poisoning of foods will continue to be revealed and corporations that proceed to manufacture and market dangerous foods will "fall." They need to change their ways, or they will fall. Do you realize the significance of the impact of these lowest of vibrational foods on your bodies? It is the main cause of disease, and no country remains untouched, although some are much more affected than others.*

Note: While in a lucid sleep, I saw a third eye vision of the common ribbon we see to bring awareness to a cause, usually disease. This was a signal to bring up the extreme usage of the ribbon symbols created by foundations and organizations, and greatly used by corporations that truthers would argue are for promoting them for the goal of profit, not cures.

Ribbon symbology is everywhere including in grocery stores and printed on food products that we eat—so the energy of disease runs rampant. As we know, the disease of cancer, for example, is a huge money maker in and of itself, while true cures are often hushed or made illegal. We must wake up to this reality and not further feed this abomination toward our health and well-being, and rather rise above the matrix and raise the sword to it.

Our actions speak loudly in all ways, certainly when it comes to the outside world. The days of being concerned how things appear or caring what others think are coming to a close. As we move closer to our souls, we protect our hearts and consider who we allow into our hearts, whether they resonate with our most vital ways of being or seeing, while not allowing in those who bring us down, or treat us without kindness and respect.

As Michael says in *Michael's Clarion Call*: *Always be aware of the company you share things with. A jealous person, for instance, will not serve your own growth.* Jealousy can be extremely destructive for the sender of jealous energy as well as receiver. We are imperfect beings and we all make mistakes and hurt each other intentionally and unintentionally. The most healthy and freeing action is always to face, acknowledge, and take responsibility for any pain inflicted; otherwise, the burdens continue on in our relationships and in our hearts, unnecessarily so.

We are moving into authentic relationships of the soul as personalities are taking a second seat.

This includes all kinds of relationships, not just of the romantic kind. But surely, in love relationships we are finding that the way to more successful and profound pairings are through connection on deeper levels of being. We are less attracted to relationships that provide just security, safety, often being more personality-based, and rather desire rich soul connection that is so much more powerful and fulfilling for our hearts.

In general, we are re-evaluating how we spend our time. Our work, activities, and interests that were once commonplace and routine, may no longer be satisfying. Even traditions within the family structure, community, or on a global scale are being reconsidered and redefined—perhaps taking a new look at how we celebrate Christmas as we grow our movement away from materialism, for example. As we change from the inside out, what is outside of us can suddenly feel foreign or unappealing. For instance, walking into a shopping mall or attending a sports event may suddenly feel less desirable. This is evolution as we grow our spiritual selves and temper materialism and certain societal traditions. The resulting changes can be small and personal to far-reaching and global.

Yes, our desires are changing naturally. We may find that the material things we longed for "when we have the money" are no longer desired. The longing for the material is waning with the greater Light we hold. While we of course still want and require certain things, the material and synthetic no longer hold a candle to the real and authentic. Our priorities are indeed changing as we lessen our material loads. The Earth cannot continue to sustain our over-materialistic habits.

Living during these chaotic times is taking a toll on our mental, emotional, physical, and spiritual health. *We simply must take control and take "breaks" from the factors that are wearing on us in the macrocosm and microcosm.* There is a barrage of fear mongering by mainstream media as well as perhaps fear mongering by people in our personal lives—this constant input of confusing and often upsetting information puts stresses on our brains and hearts. These breaks can be in the form of extra rest, meditation, being out in nature as much as possible, earthing, exercise, even just going into a room by yourself to zone out. We do need these breaks more than ever to rejuvenate.

When I was going through those challenges that blindsided me this year, it was the consistent connection with my Heavenly friends, and especially Archangel Michael of course, that got me through. I was constantly talking to them and praying to God, even crying for help—and I always got the help I needed to get through each day. This perpetual connection was a gift that made me feel ever protected and loved, no matter what was going on outside of me. You may know just what I mean.

Also, as we remain vigilant of all the poisons being forced on us in the world through various means, we must release our fears of their effect on health by proactively making the best choices we can, and giving our concerns to the Heavens. My faith lies in the present and often unknown technologies and advance healing modalities, and especially those to come that will restore our health, in my opinion. The worry about health ramifications can possibly create what we do not desire for ourselves, *so we must balance awareness and concern with trust and appropriate action.* I do believe that our strong spirits, when aligned with this strength of who we really are—along with sound, informed choices—will carry us through.

And we can literally send to our bodies love energy. From *Michael's Clarion Call*:

*Try something. Whisper to yourself in your mind the words, "I Am Love." Now in your mind, shout the words, "I Am Love," and with feeling. Do you feel the difference?*

Mary: When I whispered, I felt something. But when I shouted it loudly in my mind, I *really* felt something. I could almost feel my cells rejoicing. I know that sounds funny, but that is just what it felt like; it was as if it caused great movement of my cells, and energy just flowing through my body. How amazing that it is being felt so powerfully.

*Your cells respond to love—the feeling of love. When you say, "I Am Love," your cells experience the feeling of love, and this is positive energy being moved throughout your cells and all parts of your body and all levels of your being. If you want to fully heal your sprain, keep telling yourself that you are love! If you want to heal anything, spread the love around.*

Mary: I feel like I just took the best supplement I could ever take. My body feels like it is singing now. This is so simple and yet extremely powerful. My mood has brightened even more so. "I Am Love!" Certainly, it is the feelings behind it that are most important, to really feel love.

As the famous saying goes "If you have your health, you have everything." We must nurture all aspects of our health, to stay strong and vital. We do this by ultimately staying in close connection with our hearts. We will know when something is not serving us, whether a food, a person, a remedy, or an activity, for example. We then exercise our free will with certainty. And we most definitely can use Michael's sword to lead us to optimal health!

**Focus on the real:** We as a whole are swayed in limitless ways to spend too much of our time on technology, myself included for sure. Whether we find ourselves constantly reaching for our phones or computers and even sleeping right next to them, eating our meals while scrolling and searching, using endless apps and playing games we used to somehow survive without—we are being extremely and constantly programmed to rely on technology for everything. This is especially why we must focus on the real, to maintain our natural balance. Online distractions are numerous and persistent, and it's especially concerning for our children who need social and real world interaction. For us to be outside in real life every chance we get and find the necessary balance is vital—while spending quality time with those we resonate with most.

Literally immerse yourself in simple states of joy. Find every excuse to exercise your greatest healer—laughter! Walk, run, dance with yourself and others, and reap the rewards from this freedom of movement. And surround yourself with beauty whether out in nature or simply appreciating the beauty of a moment. This is especially important to support your sword work!

Yes, we are naturally feeling the urge to get back to the simple and real. Simplicity is truly key—having less synthetic things that tie us down may provide relief. We need the Earth, and the Earth needs us Light carrying souls too, a symbiotic relationship—this serves all on invisible levels. Technology is pushing us away from nature as the powers that be (soon to be *were*) continue to force atrocities on our planet. Our best response is to be out there in it, sending our energy around, literally getting our DNA out there in nature.

Most upsettingly, reports are building that these powers are suddenly thrusting their AI (Artificial Intelligence) plans on us, as they are conditioning us in greater ways to have our lives increasingly run by this kind of technology which is being largely abused and which could (but won't) result in diminishing our humanity. We have a choice in how we respond to it. The first robot in the world to become a citizen has been recently touted, and I find this extremely disturbing. Do you see how this design could (but will not) cause movement away from our true destiny, to live from our hearts?

We must maintain our empathy, compassion, and love above all else. As we live from our hearts and express from our hearts, constantly listening to the unsurpassed wisdom of our hearts, we stay out of fear, out of the dark's design, and maintain our inner peace and joy to tap into!

Archangel Michael shared the following wisdom on November 4, 2015:

*When you question over and over again the same situation, product, practitioner, living choices, most certainly your beliefs, et cetera, it is saying something to you. Listen carefully. There is a reason always. Perhaps you have a deep inner knowing, an intuitive sense, and yet you are conflicted between the deeper truth and what your mind says. You know what I will advise in this case... simply go into your heart for the answers. It takes courage to act on what you know, sometimes it takes great courage. When humanity is going through so much necessary change as the Light continues to reveal, it must find the courage to act on new choices. It is the way change can and must happen. Find the treasures of love, peace, understanding, courage, and much more right in your hearts.*

Remember that by working with Michael, he can help you *save years.*

**Let your money vote.** If everyone stopped buying gmo and pesticide-laden foods, the companies supporting these often forced farming practices would be out of business as the organic market (normal food) would explode even more so. If everyone stopped watching movies filled with violence, war, and anything that dishonors and disrespects life, they wouldn't make those movies anymore. By watching them, we are part of the problem—everything is energy and vibration, right?

This is very empowering because we can truly vote in this way. Truthers have provided overwhelming proof of election fraud recently and over the years, at least in the United States. For that and other reasons, people are finding less reason to vote, most especially in the elections for high office. Many also believe that no truly light-filled and heart-centered politician will be "allowed" to lead at this point—rather, we are left with the most impossible choices. We then argue endlessly about who is the better candidate, which only divides us further and brings up more anger and fear.

As stated, the dark continually uses movies, television, advertising, news, the Internet, and each other, to condition us. Look at the numerous, constantly airing pharmaceutical ads on television for too many years now designed to make us expect that we need drugs. What we hear so repetitively can go right into our subconscious minds and run us. We have power over this, we can raise the sword to all of the conditioning.

As I note in *I Can See Clearly Now*:

"You cannot turn on the television these days, in the United States, without be subjected to a deluge of pharmaceutical ads. I firmly believe that watching these commercials is very dangerous for our health. All the words about diseases and symptoms are being repetitively heard by our subconscious as well as our conscious minds. We are told about an endless number of medications as if we cannot live without them. Of course, some medications may be necessary and are to be blessed, but should a large percentage of us three hundred million plus Americans be bombarded on a daily basis with these messages?"

"We are being inundated with the energy of disease. Whether we sit idly in front of the television or walk through the store that promotes foods that prevent this or that disease, even without paying specific attention, our subconscious minds are still recording everything. We must counter these influences by concentrating on and feeling gratitude for our health and what is working well in our bodies."

I call this "fear pollution" and we must reverse it. We can laugh the ridiculousness away when "the potential side effects described appear to greatly override the benefits." We cannot escape it fully, of course, as it is all around us everywhere we go, online and offline, but at least lessening our exposure to the television is a great start for those this resonates with.

This book was published in 2008. In recent years, I chose to no longer watch television nor even own one as I finally got to the point where I was not only no longer entertained, but I finally gained awareness of the intensity and insanity of the programming of our minds and, especially, our children's minds, and I wanted freedom from it.

Most sadly and upsetting, even our children's tv programming, movies, books, etc., are being used to condition our children. For those who are completely unaware, this may come as a great shock, but you can research ways that subliminal messages are being purposefully included in popular entertainment for youth. Our young children, for instance, are being conditioned to accept geoengineered skies as "normal" and are even subjected to subliminally sexualized material, through movies, books, etc.

Another example of conditioning is the absolute horror of 911 where we are left with countless questions as to what really went on and who was really behind it. If we had a fair and unbiased media, the endless 911 inconsistencies would have been plastered everywhere long ago. I will never forget when the horrific "shock and awe" invasion of Iraq was played live on television in 2003—feeling immense shock and not a shred of awe watching a city be bombed for no good reason. It was shown live on television as if we were to be proud of such "patriotism," with the Hollywood-style graphics and sounds accompanying it, as if entertainment.

I wondered how many kids were watching this, being conditioned along with adults into the continued acceptance of war. Consider all the lives tragically lost on 9/11/2001 and yet so little mention of the significantly more lives lost in Iraq, as if their lives mattered any less? May we raise the sword for Light, truth, and protection onto these and all senseless and dark tragedies in our past and distant past.

What is now running rampant on media outlets is the constant purging of information and situations designed to *distract us* from the real and serious issues facing our world. We have been continuously sidetracked, taking the bait, and then often focusing and even fighting with each other over whatever the distraction is, while the deceptions, damage, and silent passing of bills into law, etc., continue on. We can buffer our reactions to what is "fed" to us. We can choose to take ourselves out of this formula *and instead place our energies on spreading awareness and raising the sword.*

**Consider straying from the popular.** As we wake up more and more, and see what is really going on behind the scenes, we find ourselves straying from plenty of the big names. Many of the big name brands, big name politicians, big name stores, big name (chain) restaurants, big name medicines, big name media and productions, big name celebrities, big name products—no longer feel right to us.

Again, in many, *not all cases*, we may sway from the popular, and find ourselves frequenting the "mom and pop" stores and restaurants—buying local. We also may choose organic products from the smaller and less known companies—and not ones bought out by big conglomerates with sweet and "natural" names to entice, unbeknownst to many.

We are getting and will get to the point where we must question what many famous religious leaders, political leaders, and certainly celebrities— even our most beloved ones—say in their well written speeches that is filled with propaganda designed for the masses, more than truth—instead of just blindly believing it all. That used to be me, but not anymore. We must check within and check out of naiveté. We must discern everything before we allow it a place in our hearts and minds.

Time will show that some of the most famous people in politics and the entertainment business, for example, are not whom we want to believe they are, *or are acting against their own accord*. Yes, the endless sex scandals are being revealed suddenly and recently—it must be exposed and healed which will further bring forth the Divine Feminine energies—and so much more must and will unveil. Ultimately, we seek the authentic. And when we do this, we find ourselves shedding old beliefs and thoughts about what is true, real, and acceptable.

Political leaders will not save us—we will save us. As mentioned, many would argue that the non-corrupt aren't allowed into high office of major countries. We simply must demand the unraveling of all the untruths and gross deceptions as this is the only way to freedom. We must put a stop to the brainwashing and conditioning, and turn off contrived and controlled mainstream news.

The fact is, we are each our own gurus. While we all have our own unique gifts and abilities—and we must always share them to help and support each other and the greater good—ultimately, we each have the power within to lead our lives best. Self-empowerment will help shift this world.

As the house of cards continues to fall in politics, religion, media, banking, the food industry, the medical industry, the pharmaceutical industry, the entertainment industry, and on and on, people are going to be in great shock. Some may simply not be able to cope and will reject truths, perhaps through cognitive dissonance; this is already happening. The truths about 911 are still unbeknownst to many—how can this be?

The difficult truths I share in this chapter, while not enjoyable, are necessary for us all to raise awareness about. We cannot be playing our violins while avoiding the fact that the ship is sinking—we must acknowledge the truths to save ourselves. I often recall my Titanic and rose synchronicities as described in *I Can See Clearly Now* which are most extraordinary and profound—clearly communicating that while we have been sinking, we will be saved!

Actors aren't just in Hollywood, they are everywhere—everywhere that is "running the show." We often don't want to see truths in our own personal lives, let alone outside of them, but we are being constantly played with orchestrated theater. Even those of us who feel very woken up—there is so much we have yet to know and understand. The insanity runs very deep, tragically. There are some hard truths that will indeed be difficult to hear about. And the way to handle them is to always view them from that high perspective. As Michael advised several years ago in *Michael's Clarion Call:*

*There has been so much darkness. Not just about what you read in your newspapers or watch on the television, but there is darkness of such great magnitude that is very little known, and yet it is becoming slowly revealed. Because of the Lightworkers spreading the Light, these dark forces are dismantling on their own. I tell you that where there is Light, darkness cannot remain. There will be shocking and upsetting news of the darkness that has resided among all of you. And many of you will be glad you never knew about it as it would have been too hard to bear knowing about. It would have ripped at your sense of well-being. But know that this battle is almost over. Always think, feel, speak, and act with love and Light. This is your protector. Love and Light will never fail you.*

*As news of the darkness continues to get revealed, do not let this affect your Light. Celebrate that the Light has exposed it, knowing that it will and must come down. Celebrate these final falls of that which does not serve humanity and have actually imprisoned humanity for so long. Understand and revel in the power of the Light, and don't look back. Revel in the win, and don't put your thoughts and energies on the fallen darkness. There is no time to dwell on it, but rather, stay focused on the next steps humanity must take to move into a Golden Age.*

These words from Michael are vitally important to heed. We are at the point where "the cat" is increasingly "out of the bag" and it is time to raise awareness because at this point we can create change like never before. Michael just came through now, as I write, saying:

*You are at a juncture now as the truths are being increasingly exposed at a fast rate, where it is both the time to acknowledge and the time to act. A comparatively small number of you will have huge effects on the whole; that is one understanding I really want to get through to you. Again, I use the word "exponential," for each of you will create exponential effects. You are supported by the Light and will become an unstoppable force. Now is the time to be brave, face the truth, and shift all that has harmed all of life.*

As we get closer to greater and more profound unravelings of truths, the more courage we muster to maintain keen awareness. We have the great satisfaction of the truth becoming unveiled! The darkness and lies behind religion alone, and not just in recent years, but for centuries and centuries, will shock those unaware.

For instance, truth seekers are questioning before the unawakened and unaware all the wealth, the gold, the pomp and circumstance of the Vatican while millions of children go hungry and homeless the world over. And the numerous scandals among religious authority, especially the horrific sexual abuse of our youth, which has been running rampant for far too long. What is wrong with this picture? And yet so many have been conditioned to accept no matter what, because it is "the church."

I think of Kahlil Gibran's most powerful words from *The Treasured Writings of Kahlil Gibran*:

"Jesus was not sent here to teach the people to build magnificent churches and temples amidst the cold wretched huts and dismal hovels. He came to make the human heart a temple, and the soul an altar, and the mind a priest."[8]

All that has been done in the name of God—those truths may be among the hardest to hear. When we really understand how deeply deceived we have become, there will be much anger and disgust, especially from those who had no idea. There is no way around this. But, as Michael says, we must not... *we must not*... allow the pain of truth to affect our Light. We have been deceived over eons of time, in our past lives which we have cellular memory of, and we must unify now and take the next steps to a new, enlightened way of living and being. We are all here exactly for this.

How many times have we heard that fear is the opposite of love. We are human and it is natural to fear at times. But as Michael says in *Michael's Clarion Call*, it is also a choice:

*It is a choice to fear. Fear is an emotion that can arise when one is faced with the unknown. There is much unknown to you about the changes before you. However, many changes have already occurred, and those of you who have flowed with them understood what was going on behind the scenes. For instance, you witnessed the economic fall, but instead of going into fear, you celebrated. You understood this was necessary. And that is the way it is.*

*Look at everything that is occurring around you from a higher perspective and you will not hold fear.*

---

[8] Gibran, Kahlil. *The Treasured Writings of Kahlil Gibran.* New Jersey: Castle Books, 1985.

*Look at all the Lightworkers sharing their messages of Light and see how that resonates in your heart. Look within and ask if you are tired of the darkness, the hatred, the deceit, and all the less than palatable ways of life on Earth that you have endured for so long. Ask yourself if you are ready for this change. And, finally, look to your angels and the Universe's messages for comfort and guidance to show you the way to a new beginning.*

*Are you understanding the scope and magnitude of these changes? Life will never be the same, and that is for you to celebrate like you have never celebrated before. If these words make you shiver in fright, it is the process of change and the unknown that make you feel this way. I recommend that you start making little changes in your life and get used to the process of change. Learn to feel secure with change.*

*There is good news for those of you who fear change. When Heaven has descended on Earth, you will no longer be triggered by your anti-change mindset. You will naturally embrace and accept your new life. Yes, acceptance will be a natural process as fear simply dissolves in the face of love.*

Mary: That sounds very evolved, that "fear simply dissolves in the face of love." We are all going through upheavals and trials that seem to be making us face our fears, temper our anger, and move toward love. Yet, we also need to stand up for ourselves at the same time, and not let others take advantage of us more peace-loving people.

*That is among your more challenging lessons, to stay in the Light while dealing with the darkness. Once you learn these lessons, you can move on from them, and your growing Light will deflect the darkness. In every situation, as you endure these lessons, you have the choice to stand in the Light and stand proud and strong—or cower and join the darkness of anger and negativity. Just imagine the Light flowing through you, your angels with you supporting you, and allowing the Light and the angels to guide you.*

**Living with dark amidst the Light.** The fact is... Light and dark live side by side, everywhere we look as we still reside on a planet of duality. Even among the darkest of situations that humanity has experienced, Light resides right alongside it. For instance, on 9/11/2001 we witnessed among the worst but also the best of humanity. The compassion that came out of 911 helped to change this world. Our humanity the world over was prevalent, helping to transmute the extreme darkness.

When we look up, we see the atrocities committed in our beautiful skies with geo-engineering blocking our sun which is vital to life while we—all living things from humans and animals to the trees and plants—are breathing in the particulates. We are hearing from some truth seekers that these sprayings are creating holographic screens in the sky for dark intentions and deceptions to come. What I do know is that Heaven is also leaving messages of Light, not only in the clouds but sometimes even within those chemtrails.

This was the inspiration for my book about the skies—to note the miracles up there alongside its opposite. *Look Up! See Heaven in the Clouds* gives several dozen pictorial examples of this, where Heavenly faces, symbols, even letters and numbers in the clouds are blessing us with faith, love, guidance, and validation—usually in the most perfect, synchronistic moments. We are being spoken to in this way. You have witnessed this very phenomenon in the cloud pictures I've shared in this book, and perhaps in your own life, as well. I created *Look Up!* to counter the most disheartening sights we see up there, sometimes on a daily basis these days.

Why does the dark use sacred symbols, names, numbers, and geometry? To confuse, to cause us to fear, or to utilize the high energy these various objects carry? Consider what was already shared regarding the all-seeing eye in the previous chapter. Also, with reference to numbers, the number 13 is used to instill fear (i.e. Friday the 13th). And yet the number 13 is actually connected to the Flower of Life and the Divine Feminine. There is much history to this sacred number and associations in the distant past.

Numerologically speaking, the number 6 represents "harmony," so 666 is harmony to the third degree, and yet the opposite meaning is most readily thought of as per the Book of Revelations and spreads fear. The number 11 is a divine Master Number, symbolizing illumination. And yet the 911 horror was filled with symbolism and usage of this number. We must not let any of this confuse or corrupt the beauty of the holy names, power numbers, and sacred shapes and symbols we hold dear in our hearts and minds. Just look at how the name of the Goddess Isis is used in our day.

We are also growing our awareness, understanding, and acceptance that we each have a shadow side, and we are now being asked to face it like never before. We are being urged to acknowledge, accept, and transmute that which is not serving our evolving selves, as we move further into our hearts. For years now, we've gone through an intense period of time where everything is literally in our faces, all that we need to confront, heal, and transcend. The sooner we are willing to address our lessons and shadow sides, the easier and more rapid this whole process.

**Consider who you allow into your life**. This is one of the most important and yet difficult subjects to broach because we do not want to live in fear of others and anyone who desires a relationship with us. However, we can tune into the wisdom of our hearts and with mere awareness and resolve, we learn to trust our powerful feelings. And especially with Michael's sword, we have protection available at all times—so there truly is nothing to fear. The sword has proven to be a life changer for me, in ever unfolding ways, and may it be for you, as well.

In these chaotic times, we are seeing darkness working increasingly so through people; *again, some are aware and many are not*, meaning they have dark entities working through them. A common way one picks up entities is when addicted to drugs and/or alcohol. Or someone who is constantly negative can attract entities, as well. So, energies can be sent through these people. For those carrying the Light, especially those who are actively bringing more Light onto this planet, we must ward off dark attempts to cause upset, fear, division, chaos, and lack of inner peace.

In recent months, this topic has come up increasingly so and with several in my life, which synchronistically gave me yet more reason to broach this topic. I know of many Lightworkers questioning why there is so much disharmony in their lives, suddenly, whether regarding their relationships, or they want to give up on their Lightwork, or give up in general, and it's leaving them in states of fear and confusion.

Some may argue that even thinking about this will attract psychic attacks. In my experience, those of us who directly addressed situations and tended to them, were empowered and made stronger. Because of my awareness of the *games* I dealt with, including those that were blatant attacks the person committing them was well aware of, the naïve side of me waned as the assertive side of me grew stronger. We all have to get real and get honest with what is going on especially as the dark increases its hold, and not allow ourselves to be affected. *We absolutely have the power and ability to lift ourselves above these games.*

Being around those who are sending dark energy, aware or unaware, can drain you energy-wise and even give you headaches or other physical symptoms as mentioned in Chapter Three. When recently speaking with a friend who was dealing with sudden psychic attack from someone he was spending time with, he asked my advice. I strongly suggested that I would simply avoid this highly psychic, gifted person who was not walking her talk and sending him negative energy. My friend agreed and canceled out on an outing he'd be at. However, his partner did attend, yet left half way through because she was exhausted! Sudden exhaustion is often a telltale sign.

As you may be well aware of, the "New Age" community is being significantly tampered with. I strongly dislike uttering these words because so many are wonderful souls fully committed to helping this world and are a big part of this community, but there are also those in disguise.

I'm referring to leaders in certain cases too, unfortunately, and that is much more concerning and shocking. They are hooking in genuine Lightworkers and it is affecting their Lightwork, often without their awareness that they are being tampered with. I have more than once wondered if there is suddenly a dark "walk-in" or some dark energy attaching to the person when one's energy, behavior, and actions suddenly shift (including with beloved celebrities, leaders, etc.).

A friend of mine, after my challenging experiences earlier this year, told me that her psychic friend who is well known in the "New Age" community told her she has never seen so many "spiritual" phonies as she is these days. Being very psychically gifted, she knows when people are speaking something they are not being. Again, simply follow your heart when deciding who you can trust, work with, and be with.

Use your gift of intuition combined with the sword and Michael by your side, always, for protection. Simply be aware if people are coming on too strong or perhaps too sugary sweet trying hard to win you over, or leaving you with any red flags! In general, be aware of red flags.

One man, just before intensely sabotaging me, had first casually told me he was from a long line of witches who use black magic. I didn't get the "good witch" feeling at all; this was a huge red flag and he clearly sent his warning. He was very adept at remote viewing, mind control, and had extraordinary psychic abilities. My lesson was to completely detach from this person in all ways, but not with hatred of him for what he went on to do, for that would only feed this energy that is harming our world. We can each help to stop the cycle. Maintaining love and compassion in our hearts is the only way to shifting our world. And with Divine protection, we persevere.

Those attempting to disturb the change makers are sometimes extremely psychically gifted and read minds with uncanny accuracy. They or the entities working through them can use mind control to try and affect one's thoughts, behavior, and feelings— they can see and then work through one's fears and weaknesses. Therefore, relationships may be interfered with as well, to create a conquer and divide within families, soul families, friendships, and work relationships. I've experienced this firsthand, as well as have witnessed the same among others.

Metatron's message in the beginning of this book, when I was enduring the aftermath of my challenges, was that I must not give the dark influences energy. Awareness of the truth is vital first though so we aren't giving our energy consciously or unconsciously, of fear especially, and we preserve our beautiful minds. We then empower ourselves with Michael's sword, while detaching and letting go. We can always call on and trust the protection the Heavens provide. And we must also do our part.

In a personal message to me from Michael, regarding the heaviness of broaching these subjects which was difficult for me, he said: *If this were an easy time for you, it would have proven more difficult to write. You needed to delve into the unappealing, Mary, so that you could bring awareness forth.* Indeed, and my challenges created such passion to prevent hardship for others which caused all of this to just flow out. And we have no choice really but to spread awareness now, to protect and free ourselves.

Thus, the purpose of this section is to help you to protect your energy by considering who you allow in your inner circle, especially. We also must realize we are all human, doing our best, and some are truly unaware of negative forces working through them. Regardless of any potential situations that may incur, we can release ourselves from the anger, hatred, or desires for revenge towards those who have hurt us. We must acknowledge these human feelings we may have, but then we can choose to transmute them. *Love and forgiveness without condition must be our focus—it is the only way to our destined evolution.*

Just today I recalled when this woman, who hosts Catholic television and radio programs for what appears to be an extensive following, wrote a blog about me back in 2010 that was quite rude and judgmental. She stated she learned that Australia's *Good Health* Magazine was featuring me as a synchronicity expert, and she didn't seem too happy about it, which appeared to prompt the writing of this blog.

This woman blasted both myself and the Jungian theory of synchronicity itself, molding together falsities to make her case. I never had the chance to share the fact that scores of readers have found my synchronicity book enriching and life changing. She blamed me for making a living off this nonsense, which made me wonder if she is making a much bigger living off of potentially damaging people's reputations all in the name of religion.

While I was upset then, I never contacted her. It actually inspired me to further awaken more to the magic of the Universe. And I am now not only neutral to this blog that's still out there, but sad for her and the path she chose. It was an important lesson for me, to watch my reactions.

Note: While working on this section, I felt psychic attack and was suddenly very drained and not feeling myself. I used the sword for protection and got right back to work. My energy shifted right away. The experience gave me increasing confidence in my power within, and in using the sword for protection with Michael right here and always. This is an immeasurable gift we have access to now.

**Eyes wide open.** Gone are the days where humanity can keep its eyes closed to truths. Humanity simply needs to wake up and unite. Bravely facing the truth is extremely freeing! The gig is up, we have been played, and we cannot sugar coat the horrors that humanity has faced and is currently facing. With the seven plus billion of us on the planet, we need as many of us as possible to get out of our comfort zones—*we truly have no choice at this point.*

Again, the big elephant in the room is the geoengineering disaster that has been going on for decades with most people completely unaware. Most don't want to acknowledge how much our skies have changed, in general, let alone the hideous number of chemtrails, seen even on a daily basis these days, that are contaminating all of life. Nothing is more important to open our eyes to than this.

So much is silent, so we must break up this silence as spiritual warriors by spreading awareness, and most especially by raising the sword. We must face the truth from a higher perspective—this cannot be stressed strongly enough. When we are in this space, we not only have much more successful results with our sword work and we are not only much better able to cope, but we are also more apt to see and fully experience the magic and miracles on a daily basis that keep us upbeat and strong.

May we keep our eyes open wide to not only the true and authentic but, just as important, the magical and miraculous. Synchronicities are indeed on the rise and we can reap immeasurable benefits from them. This very book is a testament to this. As Archangel Michael stated in *Michael's Clarion Call*:

*And speaking of coincidences, there are actually no coincidences, period. Some people don't want to believe that what is known as coincidence indeed carries meaning, often because it scares them. That makes the world too magical, and humans want to make sense of everything. And I say to you, get used to the magic. It's going to continue to increase. Synchronicities are on the rise. Miracles are on the rise. And when you desire and celebrate them, you attract more.*

I wrote a book that describes some utterly joyful, jaw-dropping synchronicities—and I'm sure you know just the magic I'm talking about. When a butterfly or dragonfly lands on you, some goodness is around the corner. When you see the same numbers, in triplicate especially, they are numerologically telling. When you have some sighting or blessed meeting with a wild animal, it has something powerful to say to you. When you overhear words from a stranger that provide the perfect guidance you were seeking, it is often a Divine message sent from above through that person. When you see signs of "luck," you are in a period of flow, versus ebb, in your daily life.

Speaking of flow versus ebb, if you recall, I began my journey to Canada meeting these small dogs named Lily as synchronistic winks from the spirit of Lillian, mirroring her desire to connect with me. And the signs have continued ever since. I often see trucks with a Lily logo at the perfect times. I just learned that Lily Transportation Corp serves both the US and Canada... interesting.

And just today, I came across a video of a small dog named Lily (of course!) who found a bird that was frozen in the snow. Lily's owner took the bird inside, blew hot air on it from her hair dryer, and the bird fully recovered and flew away. It served as a synchronistic metaphor for my surprise connection to Lillian. I had been frozen, truly stuck, and her presence breathed warmth and magic into my life. Everything shifted especially so, right after that, when I got to Lake Louise and took flight again.

To me, synchronicity is a most magical gift, even when it alerts us to the uncomfortable. For instance, when I step in gum, it's a heads up for a sticky situation ahead. Stepping in a dog's deposit, even worse. When a wasp stings or tries to sting, I am about to be "stung," perhaps by a person's remarks or something done behind my back. When I find myself following a garbage truck, there may be some unpleasant "garbage" ahead, or it's a signal to face some "garbage" I've created in my life and that I now need to release. Without exception, all these signs have always proved true somehow.

Synchronicity is my favorite validator and it is great fun to explore and decipher the signs. Before this mission was unveiled to me, I really didn't think of Michael's sword very often, except when I asked him to help me cut energetic cords, as mentioned earlier. And yet, ever since he asked me on that day to pick up his sword, the sword signs have surfaced so often, as I've demonstrated throughout this book.

With eyes wide open, we are free like never before. We connect to the authenticity of who we really are and seek the same outside of us—mirrors of who and what we are. This affects the macrocosm, seeking the real and authentic, as well as the microcosm, of course. We raise ourselves high above the insanity, and thus can cope extraordinarily so.

Nature is authentic and real, and thus has so much to teach us. When we connect deeply to a tree for example, it can be a humbling experience. For the tree not only gives us our air to breathe, as it stands tall and quiet, roots in the Earth and taking in Light—each tree is filled with Light-filled wisdom, communication, and healing abilities. I never used to see trees this way at all, and am strongly desiring to change that. There is so much we don't know, and yet this is changing. Our respect for and understanding of all of nature beyond the physical role they play on this Earth is growing.

When it comes to animals, I immediately think of Archangel Michael's prophecy stated in *Michael's Clarion Call*:

*I have something to share with you, and your reaction to this will be most positive. Think of what it would be like living as an animal in the wild. You have to fight for your sustenance. Your shelter may be bulldozed and destroyed. You are born into having natural enemies. You have difficulties that throw you into fear and attachment, not knowing where your next meal will come from and if something was out to get you. The survival rate is best for the "fittest," and the "lesser" are at a great disadvantage and at greatest risk. There is camouflage, hiding, and constant efforts to not be seen by prey. Life in the wild has generally mirrored humanity. Watch how life in the wild will also evolve to mirror the new ways of the human.*

Michael provided this beautiful message so many years ago, and back then I found this difficult to envision. But how many examples do we now have proving that this is coming true, often seen in video format? We have been seeing an increasing number of examples of normally wild and aggressive animals being unusually and uncharacteristically warm to humans, such as lions hugging and cuddling with a person. Or the numerous examples of interspecies friendships that you wouldn't expect. It appears that the love quotient has skyrocketed and we are seeing this even in our animals. The animal world is both modeling and reflecting unity and acceptance, the new and evolving ways of the human, for sure.

Just as animals in the wild are mirroring us, we are also having a grand effect on each other. The most beautiful saying attributed to Gandhi (although, for the record, there is question he spoke these actual words) "Be the change you wish to see in the world" is really the mantra for these times. As we raise our own vibrations, it raises each other's vibrations, animals' vibrations, and the Earth's vibrations, to the point that one day the darkness will no longer be able to remain. This is most important to really grasp and celebrate.

We are affecting each other every second in endless ways, in the microcosm and macrocosm. When we focus on being love, being compassionate, being forgiving, being truth—the extremely power-ful energy emanating from our hearts extends out into the world, and the world must become this. I often think of the 100th monkey effect in full action. May our new ways spread to no end and quickly. We are this powerful!

**Take a "Diamond Bath."** To help embrace the energy of the sword and further raise your vibration, I wish to share the "Diamond Bath" exercise that Michael taught me, years before I visited the Diamond Vortex. I've led this many times to blissful participants in presentations and workshops, and it can also be found in *The New Sun*.

*Do you know who you are? You are a human being turning into a human crystalline being. It is time for you to start imagining what you are evolving into.* Please close your eyes and perform the exercise after you read the following:

*One way you can do this is to imagine yourself lying in a bathtub. Instead of water covering your body, see yourself covered in diamond crystals. Each diamond has an energetic charge that could light up a room. Yet, you have so many around you, hundreds and hundreds of perfectly clear, perfectly cut diamonds charging your beautiful being. Connect to the energy of these beautiful and powerful crystals. Can you feel it? Feel yourself bathing in diamond energy.*

*This is a way to raise your frequency, for as you raise your frequency it is much easier to connect and communicate with your angels. When you are feeling low or not worthy of angelic assistance, is it not harder to connect and hear us? I wish for you to take this imaginary bath whenever your intuition tells you to. And when you do, just concentrate on the feelings. Feelings, feelings, feelings... always feel first.*

Note: You truly may enter into an ecstatic state. My bathtub is quite huge in my imagination. Archangel Michael says that you need not expect this charge to easily dissipate. And when it does, you can always take another bath!

Ground this blissful energy deep into your being. Michael, you once said that keeping ourselves grounded throughout the changes will be a challenge. In *Michael's Clarion Call*, you stated: *This will be your challenge, as you will feel "swept off your feet" in love with the new Earth.*

**Break the molds of conditioning and just do you.** We are learning to let go of societal programming and break the molds of conditioned living in this world. As we wake up to truths and new ways of being, we realize just how absolutely conditioned humanity is in endless ways that really no longer serves us. And we learn to break the conditioning with new choices that reflect who we are and who we are becoming.

French philosopher Henri Bergson was well ahead of his time; he stated: "Fortunately, some are born with spiritual immune systems that sooner or later give rejection to the illusory world view grafted upon them from birth through social conditioning. They begin sensing that something is amiss, and start looking for answers. Inner knowledge and anomalous outer experiences show them a side of reality others are oblivious to, and so begins their journey of awakening. Each step of the journey is made by following the heart instead of following the crowd and by choosing knowledge over the veils of ignorance."

We are hearing Heaven's calls into action and now. And that often calls for us to reconsider our conditioned choices, behavior, and responses. Whether we are spiritual warriors raising the sword with Archangel Michael and/or in other ways—by being truthers bravely raising awareness in this world, being the teachers and healers for many, participating in healing and prayer circles, traveling the world healing and transmuting the darkness— we will be intensely supported.

I share the following story as a most beautiful and memorable example of how magical and powerful our lives can be when we simply follow our hearts and guidance—sometimes beyond convention and common sense. It's also an example of how Divinely guided we are when we follow our hearts.

In September of 2016, I traveled to the South of France. It was somewhere I wanted to go for a long time. Deeply felt emotions don't lie as for years, I could just hear the phrase "South of France," and I could almost cry partly because of the whole connection with Mary Magdalene, but also because of the Cathars. I strongly feel that I was a Cathar at the time of their genocide.

My intention to go to France was to help anchor in the Divine Feminine energies as millions of us are doing the world over, but I was also absolutely guided to help release and heal the tragic past of the Cathars. As you may know, the Cathars revered Mary Magdalene. And they were massacred for their beliefs in the 1200s, in Montségur.

I knew that when I did make this trip, I would go to Cathar country to do some healing work. I stayed in this little village I was very drawn to, in close proximity to well-known Rennes-le-Château in the Languedoc-Roussillon region. I had no idea until I arrived that my rental suite literally backed up to the sacred mountain, Mt. Cardou (Pech Cardou), known to have great relation to Jesus and Mary Magdalene. In fact, there are theories that Jesus was buried there, and I was told that to this day excavations are occurring in this mountain to find his remains.

On September 26th, I felt strongly that it was the day to go to Montségur, about an hour's drive from where I was staying. The Château de Montségur, the fortress of the Cathars, sitting on top of the mountain was breathtaking. I walked up to the field, Camp des Cremats ("The field of the burnings"), which was exactly where I needed to be for the healing work. My timing was extraordinary. A large group was just gathering to participate in a healing circle filled with such beautiful and friendly souls. The leader of the group approached me and invited me to be a part of the circle. I could not deny that I was supposed to be there so, yes, I became a part of this healing circle.

The sky as the healing circle began

Once I sat down, well below the famous castle, Michael whispered to me to count the number of people that were there. I had to include the nearly human-sized dog that was sitting straight up perfectly in the circle, as if participating, and there were 44. But when I got to the 43rd person, my jaw dropped. It was a woman I had seen in Brazil, just a month before!

I wasn't able to speak with this person when I first saw her in Abadiania, at John of God's Casa, because I continually saw her while in "Current," where you are in meditation for 3-5 hours non-stop at a time, and thus it's 100% quiet time. But I felt an instant connection as if I knew her on a soul level and knew we were supposed to connect, and yet was surprised that we never did. So here we are in Montségur of all places, across the world a mere month later and participating in a group of 44—the Universe made sure we indeed connected!

The healing ceremony was beautiful. It was introduced in French, Spanish, and in English. They brought up the year 1212 (numbers of great significance to Archangel Michael and me, and reflects the name of my publishing company) and talked about how the Cathars symbols were the sun and the moon. It was all resonating deeply.

Toward the end of the ceremony, Michael wanted me to capture the skies above us and the castle. I hadn't been aware of what was going on behind me, but as you can see on the next page, there were many in attendance from the Heavens as you can see on the next page.

The ceremony ended and I couldn't wait to meet this woman from Austria who would be my new friend. She was completely amazed by this miracle. Like myself, she too felt she had to be in Montségur that very day. We gave each other a big hug and soon realized we had so much in common.

Her name is Maria but she considers it as Mary, and I am Mary. She wrote four books; I wrote four books. She is planning on including this story in her next book with a chapter titled "Mary Meets Mary," and as you can see, I have included it in this book. She creates film documentaries (one includes the subject matter of Mary Magdalene) and that's what I desire to do in my "new life." Maria recently led her first Mary Magdalene pilgrimage and I was invited to help lead one months before, but it became clear that I was supposed to be on a solo journey, and obviously at this most perfect time. She was a nomad then, as was I. And she was taking pictures of the clouds just as I was. We would meet a few more times that week, as if longtime friends.

The sky's response to the healing of the Cathars

Maria then introduced me to her friends also participating in the circle and this one woman said I should come to this dance and potluck they will be attending that night. I asked where it was. She said "Serres." I said "Serres? That's where I'm staying!" And here it's an hour's drive from Montségur, just a tiny village of only 50 people! She said "Yes" and that "Marcos is hosting it." I said that Marcos is my landlord! I booked this place even before booking my flight—I knew I needed to stay there.

It turns out that the wall of my suite backed up to this dance hall! I attended and all these people from the healing circle were there. That evening I learned that this group does only one organized healing event per year. They had never performed one in Europe together, and here they were there in Montségur on the very day I was there.

By the way, after Maria and I said our goodbyes, I went to my car and looked up only to see a rainbow around the sun. When things like this happen, when extraordinary circumstances come together in sur-real ways like this, you know you are doing just as you are being universally guided to do, even when it appears against common sense and conditioned living. Common sense-wise, I would not have chosen to travel to all of these countries, considering my financial situation. And yet when a miracle like this happens, you know and trust that you are guided most perfectly. It was all Divinely orchestrated, just as it was in Canada.

As spiritual warriors under the auspices of Archangel Michael, I have no doubt that we each are going to feel and experience numerous miraculous confirmations and validations of our work which will eventually lead us to our new Heaven on Earth. Patience and trust are vital though, as, again, we will not always immediately see or know the effects, but we will indeed over time.

Archangel Michael came through with this powerful message, as channeled on March 29, 2017 and as one more reminder:

*Sit tight. When you are feeling overwhelmed or frustrated by what is going on in the world right now (the macrocosm), or in your own life (the microcosm) pertaining to the outside world, just sit tight. This too shall pass. Do your best to watch your reactions or you will exhaust yourself and you need to maintain your strength.*

*Think of it this way. When a baby cries, it gets the emotion out of its system and resets once its needs are met. The emotion is gone and the baby is happy again. When you exhaust yourself emotionally in response to upsets, it often lingers and resurges and simmers and then possibly erupts again. I say this for your emotional health to do your best to neutralize the emotion. This is easier said than done. But here is the trick...*

*Literally take yourself above the situation and see it from a high perspective looking down. For one, this takes the pressure off. There is this element of emotional detachment which can serve you. See it from God's perspective, the angel's perspective. We are shifting into a Heavenly Earth even though it may not appear that way to most. And things must play out. So as they do, act as you must to stand for the Light, but preserve your emotional energy. We thank you for your devoted service. We are here for you constantly.*

The better you care for yourself, the better you will be able to make great strides in your mission as one of Michael's warriors. The more you are aware, the better you will be able to assertively and bravely address all that needs the sword's energy to bring Light, truth, and protection to, and shift our world. Remember that you are never alone in this work and you truly have an Archangel by your side throughout. Never hesitate to ask him for anything.

And now with Archangel Michael, take the sword, raise it, and find your relentless power and ability to make vital change occur. Change your life in the microcosm and you will change the whole world in the macrocosm—and vice versa. We are all in this together. And together we will help shift this Earth forevermore. Your role is most significant, please embrace and recognize this. Thank you from our hearts for your exceptional willingness to perform this sacred work. Godspeed.

********

"And when they seek to oppress you and destroy you; rise and rise again and again like The Phoenix from the ashes; until the lambs have become lions and the rule of Darkness is no more." ~ Maitreya The Friend of All Souls, The Holy Book of Destiny[9]

---

[9] Maitreya, *The Holy Book of Destiny.* Redondo Beach: Kaivalya International, 2011.

# AFTERWORD

Your willingness and determination to be a spiritual warrior with our beloved Archangel Michael in these unprecedented times is deeply acknowledged with unrelenting gratitude. We are all needed and the rewards will be great as we find ourselves having a most positive effect on the whole, and in all time and space. This is an unusual book with an unusual call. For you to have found your way here is a testament to the beauty and power of your soul that has been preparing for this role, is willing to assume this bravely, and is ultimately here in this lifetime to make a grand difference. For you are one of the Lightbearers here to help create Heaven on Earth, in a most active role, perhaps more active than you ever imagined, as one of Michael's Warriors of Light.

As mentioned earlier, there was great urgency to get Michael's new call out into the world. So please forgive any incompleteness or oversights, as perfection wasn't part of this formula, but rather getting the main messages out as soon as I humanly could. I am not one who easily asks for help, but...

With all my heart and soul, I am requesting your help to get this book out there. Please spread the word with those you know in your heart need to be a part of this calling. Perhaps synchronicity shows you, or you receive direct guidance to share with someone. If you have connections with Light-filled publications, "alternative" television and radio, online marketing, etc., please act on them too. I am just one person in this grassroots effort, and need help to get "out there" and to all who are meant to participate. We need every single one of us, and now. This is about shifting our world, and the sooner we gather in unified efforts, the quicker we can do our part to transform our beautiful Earth and all beings on it.

My focus has fully been on this book, and once published, it will be to further this message and our mission together. Perhaps I may travel to places to personally work with gathered groups of Archangel Michael's Warriors of Light, working together with his sword in workshops, having online gatherings and, most certainly, synchronized sword raisings. All will unfold in perfect timing.

If you wish to be on my e-list for upcoming notices of this work including events, classes, workshops, and whatever else arises, please email your request at alighthouse@mac.com.

The new website for Michael's new call is www.michaelsswordandyou.com, where you will find further information and updates on our mission together!

# ABOUT THE AUTHOR

**Mary Soliel** is an author, visionary, gazer, spiritual teacher, and self-described "synchronist." Her three-time award-winning book, *I Can See Clearly Now: How Synchronicity Illuminates Our Lives,* is a groundbreaking exploration of the phenomenon of synchronicity.

As a channel of Archangel Michael, the publishing of *Michael's Clarion Call: Messages from the Archangel for Creating Heaven on Earth,* and *The New Sun,* highlight Mary's mission as a teacher and messenger to globally raise awareness of the Golden Age before us.

Her fourth book *Look Up! See Heaven in the Clouds* demonstrates her pioneering exploration and visual proof of this movement toward a new and Heavenly Earth. All four of her books are award-winning.

And Mary has now been clearly led to her powerful and most urgent message for humanity. *Michael's Sword & You* is a guided manual to help Lightbearers take action with Archangel Michael to transmute and transcend the chaos in our world and co-create our new Heaven on Earth.

Mary is available for U.S. and international speaking engagements and workshops, and radio/print/television interviews.

Please visit her at:
www.michaelsswordandyou.com
www.marysoliel.com
www.newsungazing.com

Printed in Great Britain
by Amazon